Profitable Pricing For Accountants:
A practical guide to pricing strategy,
pricing psychology, and value pricing
so you can charge what you are
worth.

Author: Heather Townsend
with Ashley Leeds

Excedia Group Ltd

International House,

24 Holburn Viaduct,

City of London,

EC1A 2BN,

United Kingdom

Tel: + 44(0)1234 48 0123

www.accountantsmillionaire.club

First published 2019 (print and electronic)

ISBN: 978-1-913037-07-9 (print)

           978-1-913037-06-2 (PDF)

Acknowledgements

Thank you to my team in Ashley, Linda and Lisa. You've all been great to work with over the last few years. Together we have created a fun place to work which delivers real value to the members of the Accountants Millionaires' Club.

Contents

The profitability of your small accountancy practice hinges on the prices you charge. At a very basic level, get your pricing right and it can be the catalyst for your small firm's growth, allow you to earn what you are worth, and live the lifestyle you crave. Get it wrong and it can completely hamper the growth of your practice, leave you working long hours for very little or no income at the end of the month, or wondering why you ever took the leap to start your own practice.

In our day-to-day work we spend hours talking to owners of small accountancy firms. And, with the odd exception, it is very evident from all our discussions that they are accountants first and foremost, and not pricing, sales or marketing experts. How to price, what's the real reason for packages and whether to put their prices on their websites are all shrouded in mystery and hearsay. We knew that to help accountants become more profitable and to start to enjoy the fruits of their labour (regardless of their growth ambitions), they needed evidence and tools to help them truly charge what they are worth. This is why we have written this book.

Getting your pricing strategy right is so much more than just deciding how much and when to charge. It's an integral part of your marketing strategy, sales process, operational execution and touches on many other areas of your practice.

Given the many different sources of often conflicting advice on pricing for accountants, this book will become your one trusted source on pricing. Follow the advice in this book and your fulfillment, profitability and confidence in running your practice will go to the next level.

Case study: *Hanna*

Hanna's firm was growing rapidly. But somehow the profit never seemed to grow in line with the revenue. Her team were crying out for more resource, but she just didn't have the cash flow to pay for it. Neither did she really have enough money at the end of the month to pay herself a decent income. She calculated that she was probably the worst paid member of her whole team.

Her team suggested that she put up her prices, particularly their legacy clients who were paying a pittance. Initially Hanna was resilient to this idea. She hated the idea of losing a client, especially the clients who had been with her since the early days of setting up a practice. Every time she thought about putting her fees up, her mind would get flooded with all the reasons she shouldn't. Then there never seemed to be enough hours in the day to get started on sorting out her pricing.

After 6 months of earning very little from her business and working incredibly hard, Hanna knew something had to change. So she hired a coach who encouraged her to sort out her pricing and client fee levels.

Before she set her fees she did a client portfolio analysis. This helped her identify the types of clients her firm naturally loved working with. These were growing, owner-managed local service-based businesses. So she decided to focus her pricing and marketing on attracting more of these types of businesses. She did 10 interviews with current clients who were growing service-based businesses to understand their Pain Points, challenges and what they would value from their accountant. As a result of this research she created 3 different client personas for these types of businesses. Then she put together a package of services for each of the client personas with features of her service which she knew each persona would really value.

She named her 3 packages "Early days", "Building the team", "Rapid Growth" as these were names her ideal clients would relate to. The prices for her new packages were about 20-50% higher than what she had previously been charging. Despite her initial misgivings and concerns about whether it was the right thing to do, she put her packages and prices on her firm's website.

At first she found that her enquiries dropped by over 50%, but the enquiries she did get were of a much higher quality and she converted nearly every single one. Even better they tended to buy her top two packages and not quibble about the price. No longer was she being asked by Prospects to give them her "best price".

The new client wins gave Hanna the confidence to tackle her existing clients' fees, and bring them in line with her new fee packages. She used her coach to help keep her accountable to her plan to speak with all of her clients about the new fee quote. Over a 6-month period Hanna added 30% to her net profit, and 5% to her revenue. They lost about 10 clients in total as a result of the fee increase. But, if they are honest, they were quite relieved to have lost about 9 of those clients.

Who is this book written for?

This book has been written for owners of small accountancy practices who would like to have a net profit margin of 40+%, whilst still paying themselves a commercial salary. Most of the guidance in this book is still applicable to bigger size practices and small businesses generally.

This isn't a book which will give you lots of heavy-going theory. Nor is it a 200 page sales brochure or style-over-substance kind of book. It is a book which is chock full of practical suggestions that will inspire you to take action to truly charge and get what you and your firm is worth.

As you read the book, you will learn:

1. How to set your firm's fees to maximise your firm's profit margin both for new and existing clients

2. How to reduce your WIP and lockup to virtually zero by getting your clients to pay monthly by direct debit

3. How to just attract the clients you want and eliminate price sensitive clients

4. How to move from a time-based billing model to a fixed-fee based billing model

5. How to avoid scope creep with your clients and avoid giving away services you should be charging for

6. How to get your clients to appreciate the value of your services and not quibble about your price

7. How to successfully implement one-off and regular fee increase for existing clients

8. How to get over your psychological barriers to charging what you are really worth in your firm

How to use this book

It's recommended that you first read the book cover to cover. Don't skip out part 1 as it lays the foundation for the rest of the book. If you are going to use this book to get and charge what your firm is worth, don't ignore the exercises or questions it poses. Be brave, make a positive commitment now to your firm, its future growth and the state of your bank account by making the time to answer the questions and complete the action points and exercises in each chapter.

The book is split into 4 parts, supported by a Workbook that you can download for free from http://www.accountantsmillionaire.club.

Terminology

Throughout the book there are a few key words or phrases used. These are:

Client: A person or business who buys your firm's services

Prospect: Someone who may become a client for your firm but has not yet bought your firm's services

Lead: A Prospect who has shown a definite interest in buying your firm's services

Qualified Lead: A Prospect who your firm has checked is interested in buying your firm's services and is the sort of client the firm wants to win.

Sales Process: The defined process you will take a Prospect through until they become a Client.

The Workbook

For you to get the most out of this book and take action, there is a free accompanying Workbook containing a series of exercises that have been fully road-tested with clients. The exercises will help you get to grips with the ideas and frameworks contained in this book.

The ☞ symbol is used throughout the book to show you where there is a matching exercise. To get the Workbook and full set of companion material head over to http://www.accountantsmillionaire.club.

And finally...

You don't need to complete this journey alone. Come and join us as a member of The Accountants Millionaires' Club. We'd love to be by your side helping you to profitably grow your practice.

The Mind Game

Despite what you may think, setting and getting the prices you want is not a rational process. Getting your pricing right rests on what is going on in your brain, and the brain of your Client. Only when you understand how we make decisions, how our mind sabotages our attempts at rational thinking, and how people buy accountancy services, can you confidently set your fees AND get what you are worth.

In this part of the book you will find out:

- How people make decisions and buy accountancy services

- The crucial difference between price and value

- How to conquer the demons in your mind to maximise the price you charge

How People Buy Accountancy Services

Topics covered in this chapter:

- How people make decisions

- The buying journey Prospects take before they buy

- The key differences between buying and selling advisory services versus compliance services

- The rationale behind bundling up services into packages

Before you can sell anything to anyone, many decisions need to have taken place. For example, as a minimum you need to decide what you want to sell, who you want to sell it to, and how much you want to sell it for. Then your Prospect needs to decide that they need your services and they want to buy it from you. As you will discover in this chapter none of these decisions are taken rationally. Once you understand how the mind makes decisions and the process the Prospect goes through when buying from you, you will be more confident to charge what your firm is really worth.

How people make decisions

The process of decision making starts in our subconscious brain. The subconscious brain takes emotional inputs and input from our gut. These then lead to us taking a decision in our subconscious brain. Or more precisely, our Prefrontal Cortex, which is part of the frontal lobes. Our conscious brain then starts to become aware of our decision and then constructs the rationale for our decision. This means that our decision making is not rational, it's based on our emotions, past experiences and emotional state at the time.

The brain is the most energy-hungry organ in the body. It uses up to 20% of our available energy and oxygen. It's for this very reason that our brain is always trying to find ways to be more efficient and conserve energy. This is what leads to, as described by Daniel Kahneman in his book Thinking, Fast and Slow[1], System 1 thinking and System 2 thinking. System 1 thinking is quick, automatic and based on our intuition and experience. This is the type of thinking your brain does when you pose the question 2 + 2 to a normally intelligent adult. It's also the type of thinking your brain wants to default to. System 2 thinking is slow, rationale, attention-hungry type thinking. For example, if I asked you to name the answer to 34 x 27, you would use System 2 type thinking. This type of thinking is so attention-hungry that when you are using System 2 type thinking you struggle to do anything else at all, e.g. walk, talk on the phone.

In order for your firm to find it easy to charge what you are worth, your firm's sales, marketing and account management processes and systems need to help your Prospects and Clients use System 1 thinking to buy from you.

One of the ways the brain tries to save energy and default to System 1 thinking is to use shortcuts, often known as heuristics or cognitive biases. There are over 175 known cognitive biases. The cognitive biases, as grouped by Buster Benson[2] are there to solve 4 problems:

1. Too much information

2. The need to act fast

3. Lack of meaning

4. How to know what to remember for later

It is beyond the scope of this book to look at all 175 cognitive biases. However, there are a handful of cognitive biases which are very relevant to the purchasing process.

One of the ways our brain helps us to avoid getting overwhelmed with information is by 'priming' or noticing when something has changed. Our brains struggle to make sense of a number in isolation, so like to be able to compare it to something else to give it meaning. This is really important when it comes to pricing. Anchoring is where you 'anchor' a

[1] Thinking, Fast and Slow book
[2] https://betterhumans.coach.me/cognitive-bias-cheat-sheet-55a472476b18

figure to a recent number. So, for example, if you lead on your pricing page with a cheap-as-chips package, say, £50 per month, your potential clients are going to be relating the quote you give them to this figure of £50. That means it is going to be hard work to sell them a package over £500. As well as anchoring, our brain doesn't look at the new figure in isolation. It uses the Contrast Effect Bias (amongst other biases) to measure it up against the old figure, and places significance on the amount of change, whether positive or negative. This Contrast Effect is very significant when you are renegotiating a fee increase with an existing client.

Confirmation Bias is where we become more aware of details that confirm our own beliefs. We will also continue to seek out information to support a strongly held view or opinion of ours. Therefore, if a client or prospect has decided you are too expensive or possibly may struggle to manage their affairs, they will seek out 'evidence' that confirms their opinion. This is why, when it comes to pricing, making a good first impression is absolutely vital. If your website looks outdated, old-fashioned or cheaply designed, this is going to impact your ability to truly charge what you are worth.

The world of business has known for a long time that people buy people and before you can make a sale, your prospect needs to know, like and trust you. This is often because of the Affection Bias. This is where your brain assumes if you like a person you will like everything about a person. This is why your friendships can be severely tested if you and your friend have strong but different political views. It is highly relevant to the purchasing process. If a prospect likes you then they are more likely to buy from you.

Despite the fact that you are probably an accountant reading this book, your subconscious brain is very weak at maths. Given that maths requires logical thought and your subconscious brain only gets emotional inputs into its decision making processes, it's not really surprising. As a result your brain uses a cognitive bias called Mental Accounting. Mental Accounting is the way our brain categorises and deals with our expenditures. One of the impacts of Mental Accounting is we don't look at an expense in the context of our whole wealth, just our current budgetary period and the expense category. This is why it is often easier to make a sale of £300 per month rather than a one-off price of £3600. It's also why a Client or Prospect may baulk at the fee you are proposing because it is much higher than the figure they had originally budgeted for accounting and bookkeeping fees.

Due to the Automation Bias, our brains are more likely to trust the answer from a machine rather than a human. This is why using a quoting tool in a sales meeting with a client works so well. When "the computer says…" your Prospects and Clients are less likely to push back against the fee quote you have proposed.

Have you ever just chosen the most popular option without really thinking? Or just gone along with what you friends said they were going to do? This could be partly due to the Bandwagon Effect. This is where the more something has been adopted, e.g. social proof, the more likely it will be adopted by others. This is why pricing pages often call out one package as 'Recommended' or 'Most Popular'.

Think back to a time when you HAD to buy something. Perhaps it was a new and gorgeous pair of shoes? Maybe it was Apple's latest gadget? Did you notice that when you bought it you identified a whole host of reasons why you really needed to make the purchase and why it was such a good purchasing decision? This is an example of Post-Purchase Rationalisation. Post-Purchase Rationalisation is the tendency to retrospectively give more positive attributes to the option you have purchased. It's also the reason why new clients, if you have onboarded them well, often make the best referral sources.

It's time to now take what we have learnt about how people make decisions and apply these to the buying journey, i.e. how a Prospect ends up becoming a Client.

The Buying Journey

When you know how Prospects buy it becomes much easier to provide them with the right information when they need it. It also becomes easier to create products and services which they see as high value, which in turn enables you to charge more for your services. The journey a Prospect goes through to become a Client tends to have 5 discrete stages:

1. Everything is fine

This is the stage when your Prospect has no need of your accounting services. It could be that everything is absolutely fine without a proverbial cloud in the sky. Or that if they do have problems they need to fix they are already working on them with an internal resource or an external supplier. If your Prospect is in this state, then due to Confirmation Bias, it's going to be very difficult to persuade them that they have a problem and need your services. They need to make the mental jump themselves.

2. I know I have some problems

Your Prospect has now moved on to knowing that he or she has a problem. Now this could be a minor niggle which they are happy to ignore, or a full-blown crisis, which they need to fix right now. They will now be consciously or subconsciously looking for answers to their problems.

The problems that Prospects will be driven to buy your services to solve are called Pain Points. The reasons why they decide to do something about these Pain Points will often be rooted in a deep-seated emotional rather than rational reason. This is because, as discussed earlier in this chapter, decision making happens initially in our subconscious brains which only take emotional rather than rational inputs. For example, a business owner is unlikely to buy more advisory services from an accountant because they want to *grow their business*. The real reason they want to grow their business will be more emotional and far more personal, such as "I want to build a business with a capital value of £1 million to provide me with a pension fund", and therefore they need an accountant.

3. I have decided what I need to do about my problem.

Now that your Prospect has found answers to his or her problem he or she will have a clear idea of the outcome they want. This could be as simple as doing nothing, or deciding to change accountant. At this stage they may not have decided exactly **how** they will solve their problem. What they have decided is their desired outcome. A typical Prospect at this stage will have very rational questions such as:

- Who can help me fix my problem?

- How much will it cost?

- What are the risks with choosing each particular course of action?

- What are the steps in the process to fix my problem?

4. Finding people to help me and choosing the right solution

It is at this point that most Prospects will actively look for an accountant to help them decide on the right solution to solve their problem. They will then spend time with a selection of accountants to refine their ideal solution and decide who is the right person to help them achieve it. If the Prospect has been engaging with you (or your content) much earlier in their journey, it is very likely that they will actively make contact with you to see how you can help them. After all, remembering the Affection Bias, if they like your website and the messages you communicate online and offline, and find it useful, they will assume that if they have you as their accountant, you will be able to help them solve their problems.

5. Making the decision to buy

The Prospect has now decided on a solution and the accountant they will use to help them achieve their desired outcome. Very often this point in the buying journey is known as the 'closing the deal' part of the process.

Case study: *Buying a kitchen*

Heather recently bought a new kitchen. All through the sales process, Heather was asking the kitchen company for a ball-park figure of how much the kitchen was going to cost. The kitchen company, refused to even give her an estimate, and told her to wait until the final layout was finalised. When the final price came through it was at least £5,000 above their intended maximum budget. So, Heather put the project on hold until they had saved up the extra money. She actually bought her new kitchen with a different company. Why? Because they gave her an estimated quote on the first meeting and interest free credit to spread the cost of the kitchen. The difference in price between the 1st quote and the kitchen Heather bought was minimal.

Key differences between selling compliance vs advisory services

Compliance tasks are not optional for Clients. They can either decide to do them in-house or engage an accountant or bookkeeper to do them. But the bottom line is the Client needs to do these tasks. A Client does not need to buy advisory services. Despite best practice to have one, for example, they don't need a business plan. Advisory services are a discretionary or optional service for a Client. This optional nature of advisory services means that your firm's sales processes and general level of sales skills needs to be much, much higher to sell them than the skills needed to sell compliance services.

As a result, selling advisory services to Clients means:

- They need to be motivated to buy, as advisory services are not a 'necessary' evil

- The sales cycle is often much longer than when selling compliance services

- If they are motivated to buy, Clients or Prospects are less price sensitive than if they were buying compliance services.

The rationale for bundling up services into packages

Our survival has often hinged on our very ability to act fast. As a result we have a tendency to choose options that appear simple or have more complete information rather than complex, ambiguous options. This is why bundling up services into packages enables you to sell more to your clients at a higher price. By reducing the number of decisions your clients need to make when opting to buy from you, you are ultimately making it easier for their brains to make a decision. See Chapter 4 to find out more on how to make your packages more brain, and therefore more buyer, friendly.

Summary

People make decisions using, initially, only emotional inputs. As a result, you need to find out your Prospects key Pain Points in order to help them buy your firm's advisory and compliance services.

Human brains tend to think in two different ways. System 1 thinking is our brain's preferred mode of thinking, and is quick, automatic and based on our intuition and experience. System 2 thinking is slow, rational, attention-hungry type thinking. In order to charge what your firm is worth, you need to make sure that your firm's marketing, sales and account management processes make it easy for your Prospects and Clients to use System 1 thinking to buy from you.

It's about value not price

Topics covered in this chapter:

- Why value rather than price matters

- How to increase the value of your firm's services

Why would one client begrudge paying £120 per month for bookkeeping and a similar client with a similar business happily pay £400 a month for the same service? The difference comes down to the perceived value of the service, not the absolute price. This chapter looks at the difference between value and price, and how this impacts discussions around price.

" *A cynic is a man who knows the price of everything and the value of nothing.* **"**

Oscar Wilde

How much would you pay for a pair of gloves?

Imagine a simple pair of knitted woollen gloves. In each of these scenarios, write down how much you would pay for this pair of gloves. Write down the first figure that enters your head each time. Don't analyse this figure or change it, just write it down.

Scenario 1: You are in the airport on a very chilly autumnal morning about to fly off for a 2-week holiday somewhere nice and warm. You don't have a pair of gloves on you. You see a pair of gloves in one of the airport lounge shops.

Amount you would be prepared to pay for the gloves: _____

Scenario 2: It's a very chilly autumnal morning and you don't have any gloves, and see a pair of gloves in a shop while heading to the train station. You don't have to walk for more than 5 minutes to get to your destination.

Amount you would be prepared to pay for the gloves: _____

Scenario 3: It's a very chilly autumnal morning and you don't have any gloves. There is ice and frost on the ground. You get to the train station and seen the trains are not running this morning due to a signal failure. To get to work - which you have to do today - you will need to walk for 45 mins in sub-zero temperatures. You see a shop which has only got one pair of gloves left.

Amount you would be prepared to pay for the gloves: _____

Now look at the figures you have put down for how much you would pay for the pair of gloves. There will be a significant difference between the value you placed on the pair of gloves in Scenario 1 versus Scenario 3.

Given the fact you've probably anchored in your brain a price for a pair of gloves between £5 and £40 in your head, do you think you could be persuaded to spend £1 million on a pair of gloves?

The answer that pops into your head is probably, no way!

However, imagine this scenario. In front of you is a lead-lined box which has £10 million in it. The box is in a shallow tank full of acid. The money is yours if you can safely get the box out of the tank of acid. You can buy a pair of specially made gloves for £1m which will be able to resist the acid and allow you to safely take out the lead-lined box from the acid.

Now would you spend £1m on a pair of gloves?

What can you learn from these examples:

- The more value for a Prospect, the higher the price they are prepared to pay.

- Value is *very* dependent on context.

- The buyer, not the seller determines the value.

- The buyer will only buy if they perceive the value to be greater than the cost of purchase.

Let's take the hypothetical gloves example and apply it to bookkeeping. In which of these scenarios would a client think they are getting the better deal? Once again, go with the first answer that pops into your mind.

The Client has approximately 150 transactions a month, which takes them personally 3-8 hours a month to complete. They don't like admin and are a VERY busy business owner.

Scenario A: An hourly rate of £40 per hour per bookkeeping

Scenario B: A "worry-free" fixed fee of £400 for month, but with the knowledge they don't have to worry about bookkeeping, or someone else to manage, and they save up to 8 hours of their time.

If you are like the vast majority of 100 accountants and bookkeepers who were asked this question on a poll on a webinar we ran, you would have picked scenario B.

Whilst this may be a hypothetical example, it's also a very real example that is played out every day by accountants and bookkeepers. Here is a scenario where your firm could potentially be charging 100-300% more for bookkeeping AND the Client still thinks they are getting great value.

What can you learn from this example:

- Fixed fees, with the right context, can allow you to charge significantly more than charging by hour.

- The stronger a Prospect's Pain Point, the more value they see in getting the Pain Point eliminated.

- The more you understand about how your firm's services cures your Clients' and Prospects' Pain Points, the easier it is to charge more for your firm's services.

- Your Client determines the value of your firm's services not you.

Case study: *Naveed Mughal, Accurox*

Naveed, when quoting would often quote low as he was concerned about losing the business. After working with his coach, he realised the value his firm was delivering AND that his clients were only interested in value not price. So he stopped pricing his firm's services based on the cost of his outsourced team in Asia. He built three new packages and priced his services on the value that he was giving to his clients in these new packages. As a result, with the next ten clients he won he was able to double the fees he would have usually charged.

How to increase the value of your firm's services in the mind of your Prospect?

The key to increasing the value of your firm's services rests in your firm's marketing, sales and account management processes. Remember, as discussed earlier in the chapter, it's your Client who decides on the value of your firm's services and the value they attribute is very reliant on context. For example, if you do the accounting equivalent of trying to sell gloves on a warm day to people who don't need them, you are going to struggle to charge what your firm is really worth.

The reality is we DO judge a book by it's cover. It's the same for your accounting firm. Remember your brain wants to default to System 1 thinking rather than System 2 thinking. If your firm's website and external messaging creates the right perception for a Prospect, they will automatically, due to Confirmation Bias (see Chapter 1), decide that your firm's services will be highly valuable to them. Here are ways you can create the right perception:

Focus the messaging on your website to the type of Clients you really want to win.

This means stepping away from trying to be all things to all people on your website. For example, if you don't want to attract startups, sole traders, contractors or landlords, then don't talk about them on your website.

Case study: *David Munro, Munro And Partners*

Before David redid his firm's website they were getting less than one Lead a month. After they had redone their website, which for the first time included an indication of their packages and fees, they quickly started getting 2 Leads a month. About 5 months later they employed a specialist Google Adwords agency to generate leads. After some tweaks by the agency to the messaging on their firm's website and landing pages they are now getting at least one decent Lead a week from Google Adwords. 75% of the Leads coming through to them via Google Adwords are the type of Clients they want to win. They convert most of their Leads via Google Adwords.

For the 1st 6 months of 2019, their firm's turnover grew by 19%

Understand and highlight the emotional drivers for buying your firm's services.

Prospects are never motivated to buy by the generic messaging many accountants put on their firm's website. For example, "we save you more tax", "we will help you grow your business", "we will help you increase your profits" are all very rational reasons to potentially buy your firm's services. However, they don't make an emotional connection with a Prospect. Here are some great examples of how small accountancy firms have made an emotional connection with their ideal client:

- We give you more time with your family

- We become your sidekick

- Enjoy your business again

- We take on your admin to give you more time to grow your business

In your sales process, spend time really understanding their requirements and their personal motivators for these requirements

Only when you really understand your Prospect's world can you truly understand what they really value. When you understand what they really value it becomes easy to find the services they are motivated to buy, and then be able to charge more for these services. For example, when a Prospect has got into a muddle with their payroll and been fined by the Pension Regulator, they will place much more value on you handling all their payroll and pension administration.

Really look after your Prospects in the sales process

Remember your Prospects are judging you and your firm on how they are treated during the sales process. Remember Prospects' brains are wired to make judgements on what it would be like as a client of your firm based on how they are treated during the sales process. Make a Prospect feel like they are really important to you and nothing is too much trouble, and they will be prepared to pay more for your firm's services.

Openly display real testimonials on all your marketing materials and assets

Remember the Bandwagon Effect that was talked about in Chapter 1? The more social proof you can provide to demonstrate that your firm is great, the greater likelihood that your Prospect will place more value on your firm's services.

Let them know how much the 'little' extras of your firm's services would cost them if they bought them separately

Prospects often don't realise how much it would cost them to buy all the 'little extras' separately. For example, if your firm includes a subscription to cloud accounting software and a bookkeeping app this could cost the client £60 a month. Providing tax investigation insurance, allowing clients to use your office address as their registered address and use of your firm's meeting rooms can all add up.

Summary

Your Prospect will only buy when they perceive the value of your services to outweigh the cost. Your Prospects and Clients determine the value of your firm's services.

Value is heavily influenced by context, perception of your firm, and the strength of the Pain Point your firm's services are eliminating.

3

Winning the game in your own mind

Topics covered in the chapter:

- How fear manifests itself (and what this has to do with pricing)

- The power of a strong why

- The link between your self-esteem and pricing

You may have already gathered by now that charging what you are worth is heavily reliant on you and the state of your mind. That's why it's easier to price high and win new work when you are feeling confident. The state of your mind doesn't just influence the pricing conversation you have with your Client in the moment. It influences how you set your prices in the first place, and how well you prepare for any conversations about price. But most importantly, your mind will determine whether you wholeheartedly embrace the concepts in this book, or just carry on doing what you do. This chapter explores the link between successfully agreeing higher fees and how you think about yourself, your firm and your level of confidence in the fee conversation.

How fear manifests itself (and what this has to do with pricing)

The Amygdala is a small area in your brain which forms a key part of your limbic system. It's got a role to play in memory, decision making and emotional responses. It's involved in System 1 thinking rather than System 2 thinking, i.e an automatic, quick, intuitive response. (See Chapter 1) You may have heard of The Amygdala in relation to the fight or flight response your body undergoes in response to a threat. The Amygdala is responsible for far more than just your fight or flight response. It has a huge part to play in when you feel fear and your response to it.

Your Amygdala is responsible for the following:

- You actually feeling fear and having a physical and emotional response to the fear

- Attributing fear or other emotions (positive or negative) to experiences you have had

- Rapidly assessing situations for danger

Given that the human race has survived and thrived so well over millions of years, it wouldn't surprise you to know that the Amygdala receives direct input from your senses. It's always looking out for the unfamiliar and for threats. It becomes hyper focused on a threat. This threat could be fear, uncertainty or doubt. When it is satisfied that you are safe and there is no threat, it relaxes. The thing is, the Amygdala initially assesses anything as unfamiliar or unknown as a threat. This means your brain is always trying to get you to stay in your comfort zone; to do things the way you've always done things. In fact as you are reading this book, the Amygdala has probably been at work seeding doubt in your mind. Have you become aware of any of these thoughts:

- Would I lose most of my clients if I implemented the advice in this book?

- I really don't like having difficult conversations with my clients

- This feels like hard work

- Do I really want to put myself and my firm through lots of pain to improve our pricing?

- This will never work in my practice

Therefore, in order to get the value out of this book and price what you are worth, you need to recode your response to fear. Firstly, you need to get comfortable with the fact that fear is a natural reaction your brain has to anything unfamiliar or unknown. Then you need to welcome the feeling of fear. This may sound very counterintuitive to you. But this sensation of fear is actually a cue that you are going in the right direction and need to carry on and face the fear head-on. If you let the fear win and keep your firm doing what it has always done in relation to pricing, then you will never be able to charge what you and your firm are worth. When it comes to your firm's pricing you have to feel the fear and do it anyway.

Table 3.0 contains the very typical and normal fears accountants (and most people) have in relation to their pricing and what the reality actually is:

Fear	Reality
We will become too expensive and shut off our stream of new client work.	Your firm's new fee structure is likely to persuade the very Prospects you don't want to win to not get in contact. As long as your firm is still delivering a valuable service in the mind of your Clients then you can raise your fees.
We will lose too many of our existing Clients if we put up our fees.	Your firm will lose a few Clients when it increases its fees. However, these are often the Clients your firm wants to lose. The gains in revenue, profit and extra capacity your firm will make will easily offset the losses from Clients leaving. To mitigate the risk of too many Clients leaving, it is worth phasing-in the fee increase for Clients.
Implementing a fee increase will be commercial suicide	The reality is that staying where your firm is right now with too many low fee, low recovery type clients IS probably a slow way to commit commercial suicide. Most small accountancy firms, with the benefit of hindsight, always wish they had put up their fees earlier.
Our clients don't want to go onto Direct Debit/move onto a new accounting platform/pay in installments etc	Until you have asked Clients and given them no option but to make the change, you have no real idea of whether your Clients will make the change. If you make the change the easiest option, e.g. by putting in place a big fee increase for non-compliance, most Clients will make the change.
All this pain isn't worth it in the long run.	Most small accountancy firms, with the benefit of hindsight, always wish they had put up their fees earlier.
I'm not good at difficult conversations around fees. Our Clients will just push back against the fee increase.	After the first few conversations about fee increases, it gets much easier. Most Clients don't push back against the fee increase. In fact some Clients may actually know they are paying too little and will be expecting a fee increase.
Prospects will never pay this much for an accountant.	Unless you've quoted the price and handled the sales process and meeting well, how do you know that your Prospects will never pay this amount?

Before you go any further, take a moment to write down what your fears are around changing your pricing for your firm. Then look at your list and challenge your fears. What is actually real, and what is just your brain trying to keep you safe?

☞ **Exercise:** What am I afraid of?

The power of a strong why

What's the biggest thing that will help you push through your fear and get you out of your comfort zone? It's having a strong why, i.e. knowing exactly what is your driving force to sort out the pricing for your firm. Only when the personal benefit of addressing your firm's pricing outweighs the perceived personal cost, e.g. having difficult conversations or possibly losing clients, will you sort out your pricing and fee levels.

If you are reading this book, increasing your income from your practice is probably near the top of your agenda. Or perhaps your aim is to increase your profits so that your firm can afford to outsource more or take on another pair of hands? Now these are two examples of a good why. These can be strengthened to go deeper and identify the personal driver to increase the profit margin of the practice. The most effective strong whys are where there is a strong personal reason. These are real examples of where understanding their real why helped our club members finally, often after much procrastination, address the prices of their firm:

- To increase their GRF to get a much better sale value for their practice, in order to fund their retirement

- To be able to afford and be able to secure the mortgage for their dream house

- To stop their partner nagging them and buy their own place rather than rely on rented accommodation

- To be able to afford to take the whole family for a week's activity holiday

The link between your self-esteem and pricing

Case study: *Mohammed*

When Mohammed started his firm he wanted to build a one million pound firm within 5 years. He'd come from industry so had had little experience of what was a good price to charge for the accounting needs of small businesses. So after looking at other accountancy firm's fees on their website, he originally charged at £150 per month for his clients' accounting and bookkeeping fees. With such a low price point he found it easy to pick up new clients.

With lots of low-fee paying clients he soon become very busy. However, he struggled to create enough head room to be able to afford to bring in more resources to help him out. It was only when he learnt what other similar accountancy firms were charging that he realised he was pricing far too low. Listening to what other accountants charged gave him the confidence to move away from bargain basement pricing to price his services for what he was really worth.

As a result of this new found confidence, and requoting for his existing clients, over a 12-month period he was able to ditch half his clients but actually increase his actual net profit by 50%.

Fear is not the only battle in your mind you will need to win to charge what your firm is really worth. The other battle you need to win is far more personal. It's about your self-esteem. Self-esteem is defined as having confidence in one's own worth or abilities. It's about how much you respect and value yourself.

When your self-esteem is higher, you feel better about yourself and your firm, but you also have more resilience. Studies have shown that high self-esteem means you are likely to find rejection and failure as less painful and easier to bounce back from.[3] As well as more resilience, high self esteem means you are less likely to be vulnerable to the effects of anxiety.[4]

This resilience, which comes from high self-esteem, is vital to the sales process. After all, to charge what you are really worth means that you will become too expensive for some Clients and Prospects. And if you are to achieve the goals you have set for you and your firm, then you will need to get comfortable with some rejection. After all, not every Client will want to pay your new fee level. Not every great Prospect will want to come on board at the fees you are quoting. But at a much simpler level, if your self-esteem is low and you don't value you or your firm's abilities, then why should your Clients? Very simply, the fees you quote will be limited by the level of your own self-esteem.

You may be thinking at this point, that you are going to have to "fake it until you make it". However, this normally doesn't work. Most Prospects and Clients can spot contrived confidence. It often comes across as fake and is relatively easy to spot. It also introduces doubt in the mind of the buyer; the very person who you want to be confident in you and your firm's services.

It's not easy to improve your self-esteem. Firstly, low self-esteem is often associated with mental health issues. If you think that you could be suffering from a mental health issue such as depression, then seek medical advice. Sometimes a clinical solution is the right answer to improve your self-esteem. However, in the absence of needing a clinical solution here are some simple ways to nourish your self-esteem when it is low:

Play to your strengths. Doing stuff that we don't like or know we are no good at over a prolonged period of time is enough to get anyone down, and doubt their sense of self worth. One of the great things about being your own boss is the ability to delegate or outsource the tasks which don't fill you with joy or play to your strengths. For example, if

[3] Does low self-esteem enhance social pain? The relationship between trait self-esteem and anterior cingulate cortex activation induced by ostracism. 2010. Onoda K1, Okamoto Y, Nakashima K, Nittono H, Yoshimura S, Yamawaki S, Yamaguchi S, Ura M.

[4] Why do people need self-esteem? Converging evidence that self-esteem serves an anxiety-buffering function. 1992. Greenberg J1, Solomon S, Pyszczynski T, Rosenblatt A, Burling J, Lyon D, Simon L, Pinel E.

marketing is really not your thing, then give it to someone who is good at it; even if that means outsourcing it to a marketing professional or agency.

Give yourself time to review how far you have come. It's very easy as the owner of an accountancy practice, particularly a growing practice, to get stuck in always being busy. Always doing something. Always striving towards the next milestone. As a result, you can often lose sight of exactly what you have achieved and how far you have come. You can feel like you are making no progress and this can bring you down. So, make sure that you give yourself a little bit of time every day, week, month, quarter and year to review you and your firm's progress. This progress review can help you realise just how good you and your team are.

Eliminate people who get you down. Everyone is surrounded by people in life who either build them up or, sadly, bring them down. As much as you can do, minimise your interactions with people who act as a drain on your self-esteem.

Be kind to yourself. Everyone is always their worst critic. It's our old friend the Amygdala at work again. When you find yourself being critical about yourself, turn it around. List out the positive or good things that you did. Or list out your positive qualities. This is particularly good when your self-esteem has recently taken a hammering.

Summary

In order to charge what you and your firm is really worth:

1. You personally need to value you and your firm, faking it until you make it in this context doesn't work

2. You need to identify your fears in relation to pricing and push through these fears rather than letting you do what you have always done.

The science behind pricing

This part of the book is all about actually setting your firm's prices. This is very much a science and there is a process to be able to charge what you are worth. This part of the book takes you through a step-by-step process to be able to set your fees.

In this part of the book you will find out:

- How to price your firm's services

- How to display your firm's prices in order to maximise the price you charge

© HEATHER TOWNSEND

How To Price Your Firm's Services

Topics covered in this chapter:

- The pros and cons of different pricing methodologies and tactics

- Choosing and packaging up your service offering

- Deciding on your prices

It's now time to actually set your prices. Before you can do that you need to identify what services your firm wants to offer, how you want to offer these services, (as a package or as single services) then how much you want to charge for them. This chapter takes you through a step-by-step process to set your prices for your firm.

The pros and cons of different pricing methodologies and tactics

Setting your prices means choosing your pricing methodology, whether value-based, reactive or cost + margin, how you will bill your clients, e.g. time-based, value-based, fixed fees or a combination of all 3, as well as your actual prices.

There are three main pricing methodologies your firm can choose:

Cost + margin: This is where you charge the client a price based on cost + margin. Most time-based billing and fixed fee billing is based on this methodology. Traditionally accountancy firms have normally charged using this model.

Reactive pricing: This is where you adapt your pricing due to circumstances. It's also the most common way small accountancy firms initially set their prices. Basing your fees on what other accountancy firms charge, e.g. a local competitor, is an example of reactive pricing. Reactive pricing is also when you increase your fee when you think the person sitting in front of you can afford to pay more.

Value-based pricing: This is where the end fee you charge your client is directly linked to the value you deliver for your client. The fee you receive as the accountant can go up or down depending on the results the client achieves. Examples of this include charging a success fee for tax planning or taking a percentage of the financing you arrange for a client.

Table 4.0 identifies the pros and cons of each pricing methodology:

	Pros	Cons
Cost + margin	• Easy to calculate and budget for • Easy for others in your firm to price consistently	• Costs often fluctuate but the top line price often stays the same • Caps the profitability of the firm • Can result in 'legacy' clients who are paying very low fees
Reactive pricing	• Can lead to enhanced profits	• Difficult to price consistently across clients • Can lead to a bottleneck in which only a handful of people in your firm can quote for clients • May lead to a race to the bottom
Value-based pricing	• Can lead to 'fair' levels of 'enhanced' profits • Can be easy to get clients to sign up as they only pay if the firm is successful	• The fee you charge can go down depending on the results you achieve for the client • Difficult to predict the final fee for the client and budget for this • Not easy to price consistently across the firm

Table 4.0: Pros and cons of different pricing methodologies

Before you can choose which pricing methodology to use for your firm you need to first of all consider who are your clients and what pricing methodology would make it easier for them to buy, i.e. what will enhance the value of your firm's services. This means focusing in on the type of clients you want your firm to service.

Case study: *Paul Donno, 1accounts*

When Paul started 1accounts, he decided he wanted to build a national online accounting practice. So he created some fixed fee packages to rival the low cost online accounting firms. Whilst this helped his firm pick up clients quickly, he realised that his good clients were after the personal service he had historically been well known for. This level of service was incompatible with his low pricing. As a result 1accounts radically overhauled their pricing structure and doubled their "from" prices. This new fee level transformed their profits, but also allowed them to deliver the level of service their clients wanted.

Choosing your firm's niche

Firstly, what is a niche? The dictionary defines niche as:

A situation or activity especially suited to a person's interests, abilities, or nature. Relating to or aimed at a small specialised group or market.

When this book refers to a niche, it is referring to that definition. That is, where your firm's particular passion and technical talents are used to cater for one particular specialist audience. Remember that the narrower you are able to define your niches for your firm, the easier it is to create more perceived value for your firm's Prospects. Thus making it simpler to charge more for your firm's services. (See Chapter 2)

Let's take some examples of where firms have chosen a niche:

- Cornish Accounting are known as experts in pubs, restaurants and hotels. They attract hospitality clients from all over the UK.

- Affluence Chartered Accountants are specialist accountants for dentists and medical professionals.

Take a look at Table 4.1 to see examples of some typical, but often poor quality niches, which small accountancy firms adopt.

Examples of poor niches	Examples of good niches
Accountant specialising in Owner-Managed Businesses (OMBs). This is what most mid-tier and small firms of accountants specialise in.	Accountant specialising in working with owner-managed businesses who are 0-5 years away from exiting.
Accountants specialising in entrepreneurs. An entrepreneur could be Richard Branson, founder of Virgin, or someone with a jam making business who only sells a few jars to friends every month. It's not specific enough.	Accountants specialising in working with growing independent retailers.
Accountant specialising in local businesses turning over up to £20m. Do you really want the tiny businesses, startups and sole traders? And could your firm cope with a £20m business? Would it get the service it requires from your firm?	Accountant specialising in local service-based businesses turning over less than £2m.

Table 4.1: Comparison of poor and good niches.

To help you draw up a short-list of potential niches for your firm, do a Client Portfolio Analysis. In your analysis look for clusters of clients who are:

- Profitable

- Fun or the team like working with

- Easy to win

- Readily available to your firm

☞ **Exercise:** Client Portfolio Analysis

With these clusters in mind, ask yourself:

- Which of the clusters are you and your team really passionate about?

- Which of the clusters is there a really good fit for the way you and your firm work, in particular your fee levels? For example, if your practice is a late adopter of cloud-based technology, is focusing on technology businesses a good fit for your firm? Or if your minimum client fee is £3000 a year, do you really want to target startups?

- Which of these clusters do you and your firm already have credibility in the external market for? For example, which clients arrive already pre-sold? Which clients does your firm win regularly purely by word of mouth and existing client referrals?

A good choice for a niche will be one where all of these four conditions are satisfied:

- You and your team are passionate about the type of work or business.

- You or your firm are seen to be credible for this type of work.

- There is a big enough market for your firm to achieve its growth aspirations

- There is a good fit for your firm's strengths and what the niche wants from their accountant.

If you are struggling to decide on which niche to focus on, try plotting a graph with the axes Reward versus Passion. Then plot your candidates for a niche onto the graph. The best candidates for your firm's niche will be the ones where your passion and the reward level is high.

☞ **Exercise:** Choose Your Niche

Case study: *Kal*

In the early days of her practice Kal was just grateful for any client she could win. But as she grew and started to take on employees she realised she needed to raise her prices if she was ever going to make a good living for her practice.

To justify her higher fees she decided to focus on a niche. As she had previously been the Finance Director of an Architectural firm, she decided to focus her niche on professional service firms, particularly focused on the Built Environment. Two years after deciding on her niche, two out of every three enquiries are from a consultancy specialising in the Built Environment. By being focused on a niche, Kal finds she is able to justify her higher than average pricing. And her clients don't quibble with her pricing.

Researching your firm's niche

In order to charge what your firm is worth you need to understand what clients in your niche will value highly. (See Chapter 2) This means putting yourself in your clients' shoes and understanding what is going on in their world. It can be very tempting to skip this step and just assume you know what they want, need and are interested in.

There are many different ways you can get to know clients within your firm's chosen niche:

- Reading the trade-related press, blogs, on-line forums and articles

- Following companies and individuals from your niche market on social media (LinkedIn, Twitter, Facebook, Instagram etc)

- Reading on-line forums

- Reading websites, blogs, reports and white papers provided by your competitors signing up for newsletters/blogs from your competitors and people in your niche market

- Attending relevant industry events, such as conferences and seminars

- Interviewing people who work within the industry, particularly your existing clients

- Running focus groups for people within the industry or customers/clients of your niche market

- Sending out a survey or questionnaire.

Your aim with this research is to know enough about your ideal clients so you can construct a Client Persona for each type of client.

Identifying your firm's Client Personas

Client Personas are fictionalised representations of your ideal client(s) and these help you bring them to life. They are there to focus your firm's marketing strategy, in particular the messages your firm puts out into the marketplace. They are useful in pricing, because it helps you identify WHAT your Clients are really buying and WHAT they will really value.

For each Client Persona, give them a name and answer these questions:

- What are their business or personal challenges?

- What are their particular accounting challenges?

- What are their key Pain Points?

- What sort of accounting and business questions will they be looking for answers to?

- What's their background?

- What's their employment history?

- What's their family situation?

- What are their goals and aspirations in life?

- What are their hobbies and interests?

- Where do they spend their time – both physically and online?

- Who are they well connected to?

- What size and shape is their business?

☞ **Exercise:** Client Personas

Deciding on what services your firm will offer

As discussed in Chapter 1, typically your clients will be driven to buy your firm's services by a Pain Point, i.e. a deep-seated emotional rather than logical reason. The initial impulse to hire your firm is always an emotional one, then backed up by logical and rational reasons to buy your services. Your research will have helped you already to identify the Pain Points which will be the underlying reason why your niche market will want to buy your firm's services. These Pain Points will form the basis of the services you offer to your clients. It is very tempting to think that you already know the Pain Points for your clients. After all, don't most clients want to save tax and grow their business? Or work less and still enjoy a decent income from their business. If your research hasn't gone deeper than this, then it is time to go back and do more research with representative clients from your Client Personas. What are the real Pain Points for your clients?

The 5 Whys exercise in the Workbook will help you drill down to the real Pain Points that will motivate your niche market to buy from your firm.

☞ **Exercise:** 5 Whys exercise

☞ **Exercise:** Pain Points exercise

For each of your Client Personas, identify the types of services they would value. For example, do they just need the basic compliance services? Or would they value more advisory type services such as cash flow planning and business planning?

Don't be tempted to go and look at other accountants websites for ideas about what services or products or software they provide to their clients. They are not serving YOUR clients. Only you can decide what services or software or products your clients will really value. It's very difficult to truly charge what you are worth if you have anchored your competitor's prices in your head!

You are now going to group together the service offering for each of your Client Personas. The likelihood is that each Client Persona will have a standard package with optional add-on services. The golden rule is that each Client Persona will have one package.

Now look at your Client Personas and cluster them into similar types of businesses or requirements. For example if your firm specialises in contractors and construction businesses, then you will have 2 clusters of personas. Each cluster should have between 2 and 4 Client Personas. If there are more than 4 personas, then either consolidate the personas so you have ideally 3, or split the cluster up into 2 or more different clusters.

You may be thinking why is 3 the ideal number for your number of packages? Going back to Chapter 1, you will recall that our brains can't cope with the amount of information it is required to take in. It wants information in an easy-to-digest format, and prefers simple, unambiguous decisions to complex, open-ended decisions. Science has shown that 3 is normally the optimum number of pricing packages for one particular market you service. However, you may find that 2 or 4 rather than 3 is the optimum number of pricing packages for your firm.

☞ **Exercise:** Choose your packages

Now you have chosen your packages you need to give them a meaningful name. Calling them bronze, silver, gold, platinum just doesn't cut it. If you don't give each package a meaningful name and short description of who it is for, it becomes harder for your Prospects to decide which is the right package for them. Remember, if you are going to charge what you are really worth, you need to remove any barriers or friction to your Prospect being able to take a quick decision to work with your firm.

For example if your main audience is local growing businesses, how about these as meaningful names for your pricing packages:

- New into business

- Early growth

- Rapid growth

Case study: *Suzy*

Suzy's typical clients were local small owner-managed businesses, who were normally between 5 and 10 years from wanting to exit. She realised her clients were either husband and wife businesses, typically under £250k in turnover who were happy to 'tick over'. Or her clients were starting to think about how to increase the capital value of their business in readiness for exit. So she decided on three packages and called them:

The Basics: This package is for business owners who are typically under £250k in turnover and want someone to do the compliance stuff for them, so they can enjoy more time enjoying life rather than working.

Maximising capital value: This package is for business owners who are typically over £250k in turnover and starting to think about how to maximise the capital value of their business ready for exit in 5-10 years time.

Preparing for exit: This package is for business owners who want to exit their business in the next 3 years, but achieve the best possible sales price.

Choosing your prices

Now you've chosen your service offerings for each of your Client Personas, it's time to consider what you charge them and how you will charge them.

Before you consider your actual prices you need to decide on your pricing mechanism. Will you charge them a fixed price? Bill them based on time? Or just charge a success fee? At this point your brain may tell you to do what you've always done OR change your pricing mechanism to what the market is telling you to do. Don't just go for the first option in your mind. What you need to do is draw up a table for each Client Persona from a client perspective of what is valuable to them, and also from your firm's perspective of what is valuable for you.

For example, if one of your Client Personas is a small "husband and wife" owned growing business which is typically between £100-500k turnover, your table may look a little like Table 4.2

What the Client values	What the firm values
Preserving cash flow - no big unexpected bills	Low WIP and lock up
Predictable billing	Monthly recurring income
Automated payments	Automated billing and payments
Minimising tax bill	Being able to bill by value
Reduce financial admin	
Knowing what income they can take out the business each month	

Table 4.2: Which billing mechanism to use

Now look at your table, and see how you should bill your client. For this Client Persona it makes sense to:

- Charge the client a fixed fee for their compliance services which is split into 12 monthly instalments

- Provide the client with a rate card for ad hoc services such as certificates for mortgage companies

- Bundle their software costs into their monthly payment

- For ad hoc services such as cash-flow planning or profit improvement planning charge the client a fixed fee with a success fee if the client achieves their objectives

Now you know HOW you are going to bill your client, it's time to set your actual prices. At this point, your brain, as a result of the anchoring effect, is naturally primed to suggest prices which are either similar to your existing prices or a peer's prices. Try to forget about your current or your peer's pricing for a moment. It's time to go and look at your personal goals and your business goals. These goals should drive your ideal pricing.

For example, if you want to be achieving a 40% net profit margin, at current forecasts, what would the pricing of your packages need to be pitched at? In order to answer this question you may need to play around with some scenarios in a spreadsheet.

There are a few caveats with this method of setting your fees:

- If your pricing is wildy different to your existing pricing, your brain will already be telling you this is a mistake and your clients will never accept this fee level. This is just your friend, your Amygdala, sabotaging your attempts to charge what your firm is really worth.

- Focus groups are not a good way of testing out new proposed fee levels. What people say in a focus group about whether they would pay a certain amount is often very different to what they would do in real life. The best way to test your new proposed pricing is to quote live in a business development meeting.

- If many of your clients are paying fees which are materially different to what you want to charge them, you may need to increase their fees in stages rather than in one big jump.

Case study: *Faisal*

One of Faisal's best clients asked him to act as a part time Finance Director and personal coach. Whilst Faisal was flattered to be asked, he had no idea what to charge his client for these extra 'advisory' services. After he had scoped the work, he realised it would take him 2 days a month to deliver.

On the one hand he wanted to win the work, but on the other hand he didn't want to go too cheap. He had a figure in mind, £750 a month, but felt it was probably on the low side. So his coach challenged him to think about the value he was giving to his client, but also what the alternatives were for his client. For example, how much would his client pay if he brought in a part time Finance Director or external coach?

Faisal realised that if his client worked with the local franchised business coach AND an outsourced finance director, his client would be easily paying upwards of £2500 a month. Plus he would be helping his client increase his net profits from £100k to nearly £300k in a 12 month period. As a result, Faisal quoted £2475 + VAT, and his client agreed the price without any hesitation. This one conversation with his coach, more than paid for his coach's services for the next 12 months.

Once you have decided on a price point which will be still be seen as good value for your current and future clients, it's time to benchmark your fee levels against your peers. But, don't be tempted to adjust your proposed fee levels to match your peers. Being more expensive than your peers is not normally as much of a problem as you may think it is. However, if you are significantly more expensive than what the marketplace thinks is good value you may need to readjust the contents of your proposed package of services to up the perceived value of what you are offering.

☞ **Exercise:** Choose your prices

It's very easy at this point to get caught up in analysis and never quite make a decision on what your fee levels should be. But, be brave, take a decision on what your new fee levels should be and test these out with current clients and in business development meetings with Prospects. If you have pitched your fees too high, which is probably unlikely, then ease your fee levels down, until you find a price point where your Prospects are prepared to pay it and you get the fees your firm deserves.

Case study: *Paul Miller, Cornish Accounting*

Paul was getting 10-20 Leads a month. After discussing his pricing with the members of The Accountants Millionaires' Club Advisory Board, he realised he was beneath their pricing for his equivalent packages. So he upped the monthly cost of each package by £25 - 50 per month. He found the higher fee made no difference to the amount of work he was winning.

Summary

Bundling up your firm's services into packages is a great way to removing any buying friction and makes it easier for Prospects to buy from you. The most effective packages are built around your firm's Client Personas and named in a way which helps Prospects self-select the package they require. The ideal number of packages is between 2 and 4 per different type of client.

5

How To Display Your Firm's Prices On Your Website and Marketing Collateral

Topics covered in this chapter:

- The rationale for displaying your prices openly on your website

- How your website can help you increase the perceived value of your firm's services

Now you've set your prices it's time to display them to your Prospects. The 'software as a service' (SAAS) industry has done a large body of research on how to display your prices. This chapter looks at the findings from the SAAS industry and what it means for your own website and marketing collateral.

The rationale for displaying your prices openly on your website

Before the rise of social media and the internet, most business owners used to know one or two accountants at most. Now everyone knows, through the power of the internet, that they are just one click away from finding an accountant. As a result Prospects' buying behaviours have changed.

But, let's look at first what hasn't changed with Prospects' buying behaviour. The journey that a buyer goes – as identified by Neil Rackham, one of the founders of SPIN selling, back in the 70s – hasn't changed. There are still defined stages that any Prospect will go through in order to become a loyal client.

These stages are:

1. **Everything is fine in my world.** Admittedly in today's fast-paced world unless you sell a particularly distressed service

such as insolvency, people and in particular business owners, are rarely in this space.

2. **I know I have some problems.** Most business owners you meet will be in this space. This may be a minor niggle or a full blown crisis. At this point in the buying journey, your Prospect will be actively researching their problem and trying to understand whether they can safely ignore it, or whether they need to do something about it.

3. **I have decided what to do about my problems.** At this stage, your business owner is now motivated to do something about their problems. They have identified their ideal outcome. At this stage, they start asking very rational questions. Such as 'how much will it cost?', 'what needs to happen?", 'how long will it take?', 'what's involved?'. At this stage, the business owner may have some ideas about what the solution is, but may not. But it is at this stage your buyer is starting to want to know the likely fees you will charge them.

4. **Finding people to help solve my problem.** The business owner – if they need to – will now start to reach out and contact the accountants they believe can help them. They want to know at this stage whether the accountant is credible and is a right fit for what they want to do.

5. **Taking the decision to buy.** The business decides on which accountancy firm owner to engage.

Before social media and the internet radically changed how people seek and find accountants, Prospects would typically identify themselves at the "I have decided what to do about my problems" stage. If you look at the Google Zero Moment of Truth research and subsequent research studies by Forrester, they all point to the fact that buyers are now contacting potential suppliers when they are 50-80% of the way through their buying process. I.e. this means that instead of coming to you, the accountant, earlier in their buying process they are coming to you at the "finding people to help solve my problem". This has big implications for whether you decide to put your fees on your website or not.

This means that before they contact you, any Prospects will have done most of their research on what they want or need. As a result, your website and social media presence needs to help them with this earlier research and in doing so, building up their trust in you and your firm. This means so much more than publishing a list of services that your firm offers. This means having a useful and regularly updated blog which answers most if not all of the questions your Prospect is likely to have before they decide to use your firm's services. Think of your website as actually the first sales meeting you will have with a Prospect.

Remember, your Prospects want to have answered all the questions they have in the *"I have decided what to do about my problems"* stage of their buying journey. The firms which have been honest and transparent with these questions will be the firms which potential Prospects trust the most. It's these firms, regardless of their location in the UK, that will get a phone call or email requesting a meeting to talk further.

One of the big questions they will be seeking to answer is how much is this going to cost. They will only get this from an existing client referral or a referral from someone who knows your fees, or if you put your prices on your website. If your website doesn't at least give them an indication of how much your firm will cost then they will go elsewhere. After all, consider the last time you needed to make a big complex purchase. Did you have the patience to keep digging to find the prices of a supplier? Did you avoid talking to the supplier just in case they were too expensive for you? After all no-one likes being embarrassed by having to admit that a supplier is outside their budget. Or did you just move onto the next possible supplier? If you are like the vast majority of the 300+ accountants who have answered this question in a webinar we have run, the likelihood is that unless you had a really strong recommendation/referral you just moved onto the next supplier.

Chapter 1 of the book talked about anchoring. This is a behavioural bias, where the brain places a disproportionately high weight on a 'primed' number. If you haven't primed a potential fee level with a Prospect before you speak to them, i.e. your prices on your firm's website, they will come into the sales meeting with you with their own number of what they want to pay in their head. This is the number that they are likely to have allocated mentally as their budget for their accounting services. If your proposed fee level in the meeting is much higher than this number, you are unlikely to win their business. Therefore, if you want to avoid price-sensitive Prospects who push back against your proposed fees, then you need to mention fees first. The most effective way to do this is to have them on your firm's website. That way you also eliminate the Prospects who are not a good fit for your firm from making contact with you.

Case study: *Ismail*

When Ismail took the decision to display his package prices on his firm's website he was initially reluctant to do so. He was worried that it may put off the type of clients he wanted to attract. So in the 3 months before he changed his website to display his packages and pricing, he measured the following:

- Number of enquiries

- Number of enquiries suitable for progressing to client

- Time for an enquiry to become a client

- Average fee per new client

In the 3 months after he put his fees on his firm's website the average fee had increased by 50%, with most of his new clients opting for his middle package. Whilst his number of enquiries had reduced by 33%, the enquiries he got were all good for the firm. He also stopped getting phone calls from Prospects just wanting to know "what it would cost for a set of year end accounts". It wasn't just the quality of the enquiries which improved, it was the time it took to convert a Prospect. Unlike before, he found that most Prospects verbally agreed to become a client of the firm during the first Sales Meeting.

What is stopping you putting your firm's pricing on your website?

You've now read the science and the rationale for putting your firm's pricing on your firm's website. So, what's stopping you from putting your pricing on your firm's website? After all, logically it makes so much sense to have them on the website. Unfortunately, as discovered in Chapter 1, humans are NOT logical creatures; very much driven by emotions, particularly fears. Whether you like it or not, fear is very much stopping you from putting your firm's prices openly on your website, and therefore, truly charging what you are worth. These are some of the very common fears:

If I put our fees on our firm's website my competitors will know what we are charging. Let's be brutally honest here, your competitor already probably knows what you are charging. They may not have mystery shopped your firm, but they will have a real sense of your fee levels from talking to Clients of your firm. But stop worrying about your competitors, there is always plenty of good business to be had by accountancy firms who do a good job for their Clients. For example, Xero did some research in 2019 where they identified that in the UK 27% of new business owners want a new accountant. If your Clients believe that they get great value for the service you provide them, they are not going to be tempted over to a local competitor who is undercutting your pricing.

Our firm will miss out on good Prospects if our pricing is perceived to be too high. This assumption is based on the premise that you will be able to use your great sales skills to upsell your Prospect to your price point, regardless of the budget they have in mind for their accounting and bookkeeping fees. Can you see the amount of incorrect assumptions here? Unless you are a very good salesperson it is very difficult to upsell someone who wants to buy a Ford to a Rolls Royce car. Without wanting to be unduly negative, but it is rare to find an accountancy firm owner with this level of sales skills. Remember in Chapter 1, the cognitive bias of Mental Accounting. Your Prospects already have a figure they want to pay monthly for their accounting costs. If your firm's fees are wildly different to this figure, you and your Prospect are just wasting each other's time in a new business conversation. Actually the opposite is true if you don't put your firm's prices on your firm's website. Good Prospects are likely to go and talk to the firms that do have a sense of their fees on their website. Your firm is likely to be left with the price sensitive Prospects who are shopping around for a deal.

We tried putting our fees on our website but got better results when we took our prices off. Putting an indication of your firm's fees on your website will result in the number of enquiries for your firm going down. What doesn't actually go down is the number of high quality enquiries. You just lose the type of Prospects who are not a good fit for your firm. But, typically in this scenario the problem isn't with putting your firm's fees on your website, it's with your firm's ability to convert a Prospect into a Client. That's why in Chapter 7 this book does a deep dive into how to create value for a Prospect in the sales process.

Experts who I rate are advising to not put my firm's fees on my firm's website. Pricing is such an emotive topic; people have strong views about whether firms should give an indication of their prices on their website. There will always be folks who say they got better results by NOT putting their fees on their website. However, you just don't know how good their sales and marketing skills are. Nor how they measured their results of NOT putting their fees on their website. There is only one way to find out whether putting your fees on your website gets your firm better results; test it out.

☞ **Exercise:** What is stopping me from displaying my firm's fees on my firm's website?

Remember, if after doing the exercise and reading this chapter, you are *still* reluctant to put your fees on your website, and decide not to display your prices on your website, the following will happen.

- You will spend significantly more time dealing with price-sensitive Prospects who are "ringing around for a quote"

- You will waste time qualifying out unsuitable Prospects who approach your firm.

- You may have the awkward conversation with a Prospect who realises that you are just too expensive for them.

Do you really have the time to waste?

Given that your website is now taking the place of a first sales meeting with a client, it is now worth digging deeper into what you need to have on your website to truly charge what your firm is worth.

How your website can help you increase the perceived value of your firm's services

Your website is now taking the place of the traditional first sales meeting with a Prospect. This means it needs to:

- Demonstrate the value of working with your firm

- Show your firm works with people like them who have similar challenges and aspirations

- Make a great and lasting first impression

- Give Prospects a feel for what it would be like working with your firm

- Instil the idea in your Prospects that your firm can be trusted to deliver

- Make it easy for your Prospects to take the next step and get in contact with your firm

- Give the Prospect a sense of whether your firm is the equivalent of buying a Ford Car or a Rolls Royce

- Answer the common questions Prospects have, i.e. Can they do the job? What's it likely to cost? Do I think we can work together?

Ask a friend to take a critical look at your firm's website, does it do all of the above?

☞ **Exercise:** Website Critique

This means your firm's website needs:

- Testimonials from your clients demonstrating the ROI and value of your firm's services

- To shout about your firm's niche and specialisms

- To be up-to-date and easy to read and use

- Bios and photos from all your client-facing members of the team

- Gives a first impression that automatically inspires trust in your firm

- To include your contact details on the top right hand side of each page

- To be written in a way which engineers an emotive response to how you help your clients

It's not just about the words you use on your firm's website, it's also about how you display your prices that matters. First and foremost, your website shouldn't replace the need for a new business conversation with a Prospect. Using tools to help your Prospects build their own quote, such as Practice Ignition's web connector tool, are great for tech savvy clients, but should form the start of a dialogue between you and the Prospect, otherwise you could be missing out on opportunities to upsell the Prospect to services they really need.

When you display your prices you are aiming to give your Prospect a sense of whether they are buying a Ford, a BMW or a Rolls Royce, i.e. a ball-park figure for what it is going to cost. You are not aiming to give them a final price on what it will cost to work with you. That's what your new business meeting is there to do. This means prefixing any pricing on your website with the words "from", so if you have a Growing Business Package, to price it as "from £149".

When it comes to displaying your pricing packages on your website, you can influence what your Prospects are most likely to buy by doing the following:

- Labelling the package you most want your Prospects to buy as "most popular". (See Chapter 1 for more on the Bandwagon effect)

- Displaying your packages side by side in order of highest to lowest.[5]

Charm pricing is where you round down your ideal pricing so the number ends with a 9 or possibly a 7. It has been shown to significantly increase sales when the Prospect has limited information about a product.[6] The reason why it is believed to work is due to the way consumers typically read numbers, i.e. from left to right. This is called the left-digit effect. When buyers do this and read numbers quickly, such as if they are scanning your website, the brain interprets £499 as nearer to £400 than 500. This is a classic example of system 1 thinking, where your brain is tricking you into thinking the price seems lower, and therefore, more affordable and appealing.

Summary

Your Prospects will want to know whether hiring your firm is the equivalent of buying a Ford, BMW or Rolls Royce. This means putting on your firm's website an indication of your fee level, for example, talking about "from" prices.

Your first meeting with a Prospect is typically when they read your firm's website. To help you maximise your chance of a Prospect becoming a high quality Lead for your firm, make sure your website answers all their likely questions.

---

[5] https://archive.ama.org/Archive/AboutAMA/Pages/AMA%20Publications/AMA%20Journals/Journal%20of%20Marketing%20Research/TOCs/SUM_2012.5/influence-of-price-presentation.aspx
[6] https://link.springer.com/article/10.1023%2FA%3A1023581927405

How to raise the value of your firm's services to your prospects

In Chapter 2 you discovered that value is relative and is set by the buyer not the seller. This part of the book examines how to raise the value of your services to your Prospects through your Sales Process.

6

Creating value through the Sales Process

Topics covered in this chapter:

- What is the Sales Process?

- How to structure your Sales Process to increase the perceived value of your firm's services

- How to run a new business meeting in order to maximise the perceived value of your firm's services

Chapter 2 of the book looked at the difference between price and value. The Sales Process is a big influencer on the perceived value of your firm's services. Therefore, this chapter looks at what is the Sales Process and how to use your Sales Process to create value.

What is the Sales Process?

The Sales Process is a path that you take your Prospects on, to convert them from someone who is looking to change accountant through to finally signing up for your services. The most effective Sales Processes will be designed to help Prospects go through their Buying Journey (See Chapter 5) as quickly and efficiently as possible. Because of the complexities of the services that you offer you need to make this process as simple and as uncomplicated as possible. Making it easy for the Prospect to make a decision and ensure that it is a lasting commitment.

A structured Sales Process will help you create the value that you want your Prospects to perceive. Defining your firm's standard Sales Process and consistently applying it for every Lead will eliminate mistakes and ensure that your firm is maximising the perceived value of your firm's services throughout the Sales Process.

Many organisations have Sales Processes in place and those that do consistently outperform those that do not. With a process to follow, everyone in the team knows the best way to achieve the results and therefore you can predict the outcome more accurately to ensure that you hit your desired goals and targets.

Your process must be repeatable and systemised so that everyone in your firm knows exactly where you are with each Lead as they move through your pipeline. Think of every Lead as a drop of water going through a pipe to your sink. Turn the tap on, then you'll have loads of new clients. Turn it off then the number of new clients will dwindle, but also beware of leaky pipes as not every Lead that you nurture will become a Client. With a robust process in place you can monitor the 'leaks' and put systems in place to recover the dropouts.

The Sales Process starts when a Prospect engages with you, or you with them, in any way shape or form. This could be any of the following

- Following you on social media

- Downloading content from your website

- Enquiry via phone or email

- Networking event

- Training or marketing event

Typically most Sales Processes have 6 steps:

1. Prospecting

2. Initial enquiry

3. Qualification

4. Sales Meeting

5. Handling objections

6. Follow-up

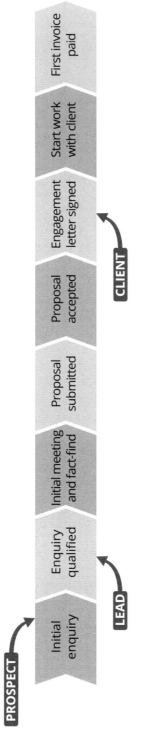

7.0 The Sales Process

Prospecting

First up, let's look at Prospecting. This is where you need to let people know all about you and become aware of what you do and how you are better than your competitors. This is also the point where you need to let your potential Prospects know whether they would be buying the accounting equivalent of a Ford, BMW or Rolls Royce (by putting an indication of your prices on your firm's website). (See Chapter 1 and 5)

If you fail at this stage to establish an idea of the likely cost of your firm's services, you are going to miss out on great potential clients who go to other firms who are more transparent with their pricing. In addition, you will fail to deter Prospects who are a poor fit from your firm from making contact with your firm and wasting your firm's valuable time as you engage with them in the Sales Process.

Initial enquiry

Your new Prospect is looking for a service that you provide and you are now on their radar. The chances are your new Prospect will be checking you out on the internet. They may have seen a post of yours, read your website, seen a blog on LinkedIn or be following you on Facebook or Twitter. See Chapter 5 for guidance on how to use your firm's website to help your Prospects understand the value of your firm's services.

From this activity, they may fill out an enquiry form on your website or get in touch with you via email or one of the software vendors' directory of accountants. As an aside, both Xero and Quickbooks provide a directory of certified accountants for their software which can be a useful source of good quality Leads for your practice. To give you an idea of how powerful these software vendor directory listings are, Xero found in 2019 that on average, their directory generated 60+ leads per month per Xero partner listed.

A great way to make it easy for them to get in touch and book an initial call is to use an automated meetings booking system such as AcuityScheduling or Calendly. This gives your Prospects a link to your diary (or anyone in the team if needed) so that they can book a slot for a call. You can control the duration of the call and it links to your diary so if you have blocked off anything they will not be given that option. It can also be used to remind them of the meeting and send texts etc.

Using an automated meetings booking system means that as soon as they decide that they want to talk to you, they can do. This can add to a higher perception of value of your firm in your Prospect's eyes. Particularly if they are technologically minded.

Your Prospect could also pop into the practice or phone in so it's important that your website clearly displays your firm's telephone number. However, it's not enough to display a phone number; it needs to be answered when a Prospect calls. An answering machine or voicemail may sound like a pragmatic option for a busy firm, but if a Prospect doesn't have their call answered promptly, it can actually devalue your firm's services. Here is why. What went through your mind when you last phoned a potential supplier and either got a voicemail or an answering machine or no one answered the phone? How did it make you feel? What do you do next? You probably called the next company on your list and never called the first one again. Even if you did leave a message, it almost definitely sowed a seed of doubt in your mind about the value of the supplier's services.

Missing a Prospect's phone call may mean you miss out on the chance of a new Client. There is no point in having a phone number on your website if there is no answering service when you pop out to make a cup of tea. There are plenty of telephone answering services, such as Moneypenny, who will become your virtual receptionist and screen all your calls for your firm.

In order to maximise the perceived value of your firm's services during the Sales Process, enquiries need to be dealt with immediately, and in a manner which leaves a positive impression about how your firm operates.

Regardless of how your Prospect gets in touch, to maximise the perceived value of your firm's services, all enquiries will need to be dealt with in the same consistent way so that your Prospect feels the love from the start and they feel they are important to you.

Qualifying your Lead

Once your Prospect has been identified and is now a Lead, you need to qualify this Lead to see whether they are worth progressing through to a Client. With the right information on your website, your firm will be minimising the amount of enquiries your firm doesn't want to progress. For example, with prices on your website, you won't be getting price sensitive enquiries and instead have the Leads who'll value your business proposition. Not using your website to screen out unsuitable Leads means you could waste an inordinate amount of time courting them to become a Client.

Everyone wants to feel special, so when an enquiry comes in you need to have a set process to qualify all your Prospects so that everyone in the practice knows what to do. You qualify a Prospect by simply asking a series of questions to get an understanding of their needs. Then use their answers to decide whether they are a good or bad fit for your practice. This is best done before you book a full-blown Sales Meeting with your firm's Prospect. If they pass your pre-qualification tests, then you book a Sales Meeting with them and the person in your firm who does the Sales Meetings.

With your team, put together a simple script that everyone in the firm can follow to consistently pre-qualify Prospects. Your script could include questions such as:

- What has prompted you to get in touch?

- Why are you looking to move accountant?

- What is the current turnover of your practice?

- What accounting software do you currently use?

- Would you be prepared to move accounting software to our preferred software package?

As part of your pre-qualification process you need to check that your Prospect is happy to pay your firm's prices. It is important to have this check now for two reasons. Firstly it sets the expectation in your Prospect's head what it is likely to cost. (See Chapter 1 for more on cognitive biases including anchoring and mental accounting.) Secondly, it allows you to turn away Prospects who will never pay your proposed fee levels. The way to check with your Prospect is to ask them a question such as:

" Our clients typically pay between £150 and £1000 + VAT per month, is this in line with your expectations?"

Before your Sales Meeting

The purpose of your Sales Meeting is to move your Prospect one step closer along your Sales Process to becoming a Client. It's also the point in the Sales Process where you give them a final price for the services they require. In order to make it easy for them to accept your final price, you need to find and create value for your client in this meeting.

To maximise the chance of this meeting going well (and you not leaving any business on the table), you need to thoroughly prepare for this meeting. This means doing your research to get to know your Prospect and their world as much as possible.

In your research you want to find out about their:

- business

- key employees

- key customers and markets

- potential Pain Points

Here are some great ways to research your Prospect:

- Send your Prospect a pre-meeting questionnaire or diagnostic to fill in and return before your Sales Meeting.

- Request read-only access to their accounting software

- Can you follow and connect with them on social media in advance of your Sales Meeting? Consider connecting and following them on LinkedIn, Twitter and potentially Facebook and Instagram.

- Read their website and their competitors' websites

- Search for their company on LinkedIn to possibly find out more about key employees of the company.

- Sign up for their newsletter

- Look up them and their company on Companies House

- Google their name and their business name.

This level of research is fundamental in helping to build a picture of your client. All of this information can be used in your Sales Meeting to really demonstrate that you have knowledge and understanding about their business, and are organised and diligent. But your research shouldn't just be all about them. Where else do you have similar businesses as a client? This is where having a firm-wide niche really helps. You can use your experience with these similar clients to show that you have an understanding of your Prospect's business. You'll be able to benchmark your Prospect against your other clients.

As well as researching your Prospect, your preparation for your Sales Meeting needs to include some thoughts about what questions you want to ask your Prospect. These questions may be prompted by the research you have done on your Prospect. A great way to make sure that all the key questions are asked is to have a standard new business meeting script for your firm.

The questions you want to ask should initially help your Prospect feel at ease with you and help both parties start to build trust and rapport with each other. Keep it simple and pertinent and remember to ask open questions, not closed questions.

Open questions help to get a conversation going. Here are some example questions to ask:

- What are you hoping to get out of this meeting today?

- What prompted you to come for this meeting today?

- Why did you start your business? And how does your current reality match up?

- What are the three main Pain Points in your business today?

- If you had a magic wand, what would you do to get to where you want to be?

Structuring the Sales Meeting:

To help you and your firm get the best possible result from this meeting, follow this structure:

Before you meet:

- Agree time, agenda, date, duration and venue.

- Ideally send them a couple of pieces of valuable content which demonstrate your firm's expertise and authority.

- If you can do, start a dialogue with them on social media.

A week before you meet:

- Check the meeting is still going ahead, and re-confirm time, date and venue.

- Check the agenda is still the same.

- Ask them whether there is anything that you need to prepare to help them get value from the meeting.

- Send them another piece of short valuable content, relevant to your meeting.

When you meet:

- Introduce yourself very briefly, i.e. in under a minute.

- Things may have changed since you last checked, so clarify how much time they have for the meeting, that the agenda is still appropriate, and what they want to achieve by the end of the meeting.

- Explain that you are keen to understand more about them, and the organisational reasons behind this meeting taking place, particularly what has motivated them to talk to you about becoming their accountant.

- Allocate at least 50% of the meeting time to listen and to explore their problems.

- Summarise to check understanding of what you are hearing.

- Identify the risks for the client of doing nothing, plus the value your firm can bring to the client by working with them.

- Find out the criteria that they will use to select a new accountant.

- Uncover their timings and anything that will affect their ability to proceed quickly.

- Suggest some potential solutions, and cost these solutions if requested.

- Find out any resistance or objections they may have about working with you.

- Agree next steps and ask when they would like you to follow up with them if you have not heard anything.

After you meet:

- Thank them for their time.

- Send a note summarising your understanding of what was discussed.

- Do your next steps from the meeting.

- If they have verbally agreed in the meeting to engage you as their accountant send them a proposal and engagement letter for them to sign.

- Diarise when you should contact them next.

Talking about price in the Sales Meeting

If you have got your Sales Process just right, your Lead will likely be fairly ready to buy when they arrive at the Sales Meeting. They may even start the Sales Meeting by asking you to talk through what you would do for them as their accountant and how much it is going to cost. The start of the meeting is NOT the right point to answer these questions. Before you can answer these questions you want to have clearly established what your Lead requires and values. A good way to handle this situation is to say something like:

" *I'll be very happy to answer those questions shortly, but first is it alright if I find out a bit more about your business to ensure I am offering you exactly what you want and need?* **"**

As mentioned earlier in this chapter, you want to spend at least 50% of your time in the meeting finding out about them and their business. This time needs to be spent establishing what your clients really value and require, and the importance they place on them. Typically there are four freedoms which have prompted people to run their own business. These four freedoms typically motivate and drive most business owners. These are:

Mind: A mind free from worries, anxieties, stress and fear.

Control: The power to choose how they live their life, when they work and the type of work they take on.

Cash: Money to fund their current and future lifestyle

Time: Time to spend on what they care about.

Business owners will have typically set up their business or gone into business in order to gain some or all of these four freedoms.

By understanding which of these four freedoms your Lead most values or craves, you can then frame your proposed solution and the features of your firm's services in a way that is more valuable to your Lead. For example, if in your fact-find, your Lead is talking about always being busy and wanting to stop working long hours so they can spend more time with your family, you can suggest that your firm can help them spend more time with their family by taking over their bookkeeping, VAT and payroll.

After you make a suggestion about how you can help them, ask them how much that would help them, and aim to get them to put a value on this. For example:

❝ *If our firm took over your bookkeeping, VAT and payroll, how much time would this get you back? What would this be worth to you and your family?* **❞**

Only when you understand how much your Lead values your proposed solution can you put a price on it. When you have agreed on a proposed solution with your Lead, now you need to price up what they require. This is often best done using a pricing tool on your computer. As Chapter 1 says, our minds are more predisposed to accept a price from a computer than a person. Most Leads will not quibble with your proposed price if you've identified correctly what they really value AND say something along the lines of *"the computer says the price is...."*

If your Prospect is looking to buy standard services most small accountancy firms offer, then in the majority of cases, if you follow the Sales Process as outlined in this chapter, you should be able to quote in the Sales Meeting and get verbal agreement from the Lead to come onboard as a Client.

Case study: *Nick*

Nick's firm was growing rapidly. They typically got about 5 new client enquiries every week. As a result, Nick was spending at least 2 days a week having new business meetings, on top of his normal client workload. Nick liked to confirm a fee in writing in a proposal to the Client after the Sales Meeting.

Given how busy Nick was getting, he was finding it was taking longer and longer to quote and send a proposal out to a Cient. So much so, many of his really 'hot' Leads went pretty cold and never quite came onboard as a Client.

So, he changed how he quoted, and wherever possible he quoted in the Sales Meeting. When he had a verbal agreement from the Lead to the fee and proposed solution, he would after the meeting send them a proposal via Practice Ignition. He left himself 10 mins at the end of his Sales Meeting to create and send the proposal via Practice Ignition. He wowed his Leads by sending his proposal to them to sign before they had even got back to their office.

3 months after instigating this change to his Sales Process, Nick would find that over 90% of his Leads would be a signed up new Client within a week of their Sales Meeting.

Handling objections

Even if you have done everything perfectly in your Sales Process, you may still encounter some objections to what you are proposing. People often fear an objection because they are worried this means that the Lead doesn't want to buy. On the contrary. If you have done everything right in the Sales Process, then an objection normally means they are on the cusp of buying, but need a little more information. You just need to get them across the line.

Here is how to identify that your Lead has an objection which is stopping them from going ahead:

- They ask for time to think about what you are suggesting

- They are hesitating about putting a date to get started

- They start to ask detailed questions about your firm or the proposed service

If you sense that there is an objection that hasn't been voiced, a great question to flush this out is:

" *What question do I need to answer for you to be able to take the decision to use us as your accountant today?* **"**

When it comes to objections, most of them are rooted in three fears:

- Is your firm capable of doing the work?

- Is there a good relationship fit?

- Are we getting good value for your proposed price?

When you realise this, it becomes a little easier to anticipate their concerns, and how these will be articulated. For example, if you were asked *What sort of results have you achieved with previous clients?*, this is the Lead testing your capability to be able to help them.

A good technique to use to help identify what are your Lead's objections to working with your firm, is to proactively tell them some of the objections that other Clients had before they were signed up. For example:

Although our costs are higher, all of our Clients have remarked after implementation that they now realise that our solutions are robust, and therefore there is no tidy-up or refinement necessary afterwards.

When faced with one of these difficult questions, you want to let them know that not only do you understand why they feel that way, but that they are right, and others have in the past felt that way. In other words you are not being defensive, but reinforcing the fact that they are right. (Remember the Lead is the one who controls the buying process, and whether you disagree with what they are saying, they are the ones who will ultimately decide to hire you.) However, you also need to show to them that Clients who had been in exactly their situation, had managed to gain a positive outcome by working with you. This is called the Feel, Felt, Found technique.

Feel: *I understand how you feel about doing tax planning.*

Felt: *Many of my other Clients, when they were in the same situation as you, felt the same way, and were wondering whether they should ditch tax planning altogether. They were really concerned that their actions would be viewed negatively if it got out into the public domain.*

Found: *However, when we have worked with Clients in exactly the same place as you now, we have found that they have been able to significantly reduce their tax bill by us helping them find ethical ways to reduce their tax bill, such as R&D tax credits.*

Many people think that the biggest objection is price. By the time you get to this stage in the process your Lead will be thinking about value rather than the actual cost. Price is a factor, but if you have covered everything and presented everything in a way that meets your Prospect's needs, then the price will rarely be an issue.

What happens if a client wants you to reduce your fees.

Even if you have qualified your Lead correctly, there are still times when they will ask for a reduction in your fees. Unless you are in a competitive bidding situation, this isn't a showstopper, but sometimes a very good indication that you are about to sign them up.

Your aim at this stage of the process is not to arbitrarily reduce your fees, as this is educating your Client that every time they want a fee reduction, they just need to ask and your firm will do it. You need to establish exactly the value you are delivering to them; i.e. what it is that they really want, and what is non-essential. If you can cut the non-essentials from your packaged offering, then you can offer your Client a more bespoke package at a reduced fee. Your Client is happy, and you are happy because you have signed up a Client and not reduced your firm's profit margin or devalued what your firm does for Clients.

If you don't have the option to trim away parts of what your firm will do for the Client, you may find that one of these approaches may help eliminate the deadlock:

- Explain that the fee is what it is, and if they don't want to pay this fee you will happily walk away, no hard feelings. Sometimes this works, and they still sign up.

- Restate the benefits of using your firm's services and how this will help them achieve their organisational goals and get them closer to achieving the Freedoms they crave.

- Demonstrate to them why it costs so much and why you don't have the room to reduce your fees.

- See whether they would accept a more junior member of staff working on their account, in order to reduce the fee level.

- Use a Client Case Study to illustrate how other Clients have also had doubts about your fees, but achieved great results, which justified your firm's fee.

Closing

If you have done everything in your Sales Process as suggested in this chapter, closing should come easily and often seamlessly. For example, your Lead may do the closing for you by suggesting something along the lines of:

❝ *That sounds exactly what we need, what happens next?* **❞**

If you have surfaced and dealt with objections from your Lead, you may be able to close the sale by saying something along the lines of:

❝ *When do you want us to get started as your new accountant?* **❞**

If your Lead doesn't take the bait to get started, then this means you need to go back and surface some objections.

Follow up

Your Lead has verbally agreed to come onboard as a new Client of the firm. Well done! Before you finish the Sales Meeting you need to set their expectations of what happens next.

For example:

" *When you get back to the office there will be an electronic proposal waiting for you to sign. Once this is signed, you will get an email from us every day for a week to get the information we need to fully act for you as a client. Our onboarding coordinator will be in touch in the first week to help you find all the information we need. They will also book in meetings with your key contacts so you can get to know them, plus understand who does what and by when. If we haven't seen a signed proposal within 48 hours we will give you a phone call to discuss the proposal and see what else needs to happen for you to come onboard as a client* "

Summary

Your firm's Sales Process is key to being able to charge what your firm is really worth. It's important that your firm uses your Sales Process to:

- Eliminate unsuitable Prospects early in the Sales Process

- Set expectations early in the Sales Process about what it is going to cost

- Truly understand what your Lead values and how your proposed solution delivers on that value

- Contrast the value the Lead sees in the proposed solution with what it will actually cost

Get your Sales Process right and your firm will be able to normally convert your Lead within the Sales Meeting.

Putting up your existing clients' fees

Up until now this book has been focused on how to charge what you are worth with new clients. The final part of the book turns its attention to:

- How to swap your clients from time-based billing to fixed fees, paid in monthly instalments

- How to put the fees up of your existing clients

How to move from time-based billing to fixed fees billed monthly by instalment and via Direct Debit

Topics covered in this chapter:

- What decisions your firm needs to make before you can start billing your clients monthly rather than as you complete their work

- How to minimise the financial administration involved in monthly billing

- How to persuade 'stuck' clients to move to monthly billing via Direct Debit

The accountancy profession has traditionally billed its clients for the time it has spent on their affairs. The problem with this method of billing is it rewards inefficiencies within the practice AND leads to high levels of WIP and lockup. This method of billing also plays havoc with capacity planning as you are only able to bill your client when the client decides to bring their records in. This results in a very lumpy cash flow and inefficient working practices. This is why many firms have moved to charging their clients a fixed fee for their compliance services, and splitting this fee up over a 12 month period. This chapter goes through the 'how to' of how to move your clients from billing your clients after the work has been done, to charging a fixed fee and billing them in monthly instalments via Direct Debit.

What decisions your firm needs to make before you can start billing your clients monthly rather than as you complete their work

Changing the way you bill your existing clients is a big project which needs careful management. If you have been using time-based billing for a large period of time, changing over to fixed fee billing will seem like a big deal. Your Amygdala will be almost definitely be flooding your conscious brain with all the reasons why the move could go wrong. If that is you now, take heart; moving to fixed fee billing for compliance services is definitely the right way forward for the client. And when it is right for the client, ultimately it becomes right for your firm. It can also lead to your firm being able to generate higher levels of profit than if you solely billed by time.

Before you start changing the way you bill your clients, your firm needs to decide:

- How will we as a firm benefit from making the switch to fixed-fee billing?

- What services will be part of the normal monthly fixed fee and what are ad hoc services which should be paid for separately?

- At what point in your client's financial year will you bill them for their first instalment?

- How to bill new clients who switch over to us part way through their financial year

- What technology will your firm use to automate invoicing and bookkeeping?

- How much time will we factor in (and budget for) in our fixed fees to answer ad hoc queries from clients?

What's your motivator to make the switch to fixed fee billing?

Given that the move to fixed fee billing is going to take you and your firm into very unfamiliar territory with a lot of unknowns, it's important you and your firm understand your reasons for making the switch. Without a strong reason aligned to your purpose, your firm will probably not make the switch to fixed fee billing. Your reasons are often likely to include some of all of these:

- Clients prefer the peace of mind of fixed fees for compliance work

- The marketplace is moving towards fixed fees for compliance work becoming the expected option for clients

- There is a greater opportunity to generate higher levels of profitability if you offer your clients a fixed fee for compliance services

Case study: *Sian Kelly, Inform Accounting*

Having started my practice from scratch, I was determined to set it up in a way which didn't cause me problems in the future. Having seen so many firm owners get really stressed about whether they would be able to pay the wages at the end of the month, I never wanted to get into this position.

As a result, our way of working is that all our clients pay their fees monthly by Direct Debit. There are no exceptions. We just wouldn't take a client on if they won't pay their bills this way. We use GoCardless with Xero. This means that when we raise an invoice it is automatically taken out by Direct Debit and additionally automatically reconciled.

My business model is such that my recurring monthly payments by Direct Debit always are enough to cover the wages and normal monthly costs. This means that I am never worrying towards the end of the month about whether I will have enough money in the bank to pay my wages.

Case study: *Guy Robinson, Xebra Accounting*

When I was a partner for BDO and Moore Stephens, a lumpy cash flow didn't really impact me personally. After all, we had so many clients there was always enough cash coming in and a decent overdraft facility with the bank. After a year or so of starting my practice I realised that I couldn't survive with a lumpy cash flow. I was running myself into the ground cajoling clients to bring their records in so I could bill them for the work. This was why I decided to originally start to bill my clients by instalments on a monthly basis. It made sound financial sense. I, rather than my clients, needed to be in control of when I billed them.

After a few months of billing my clients via monthly instalments. I realised something else. It fundamentally changed our relationships with our clients. As we billed them monthly, they had an expectation they would hear from us monthly. Rather than as we had done previously, at key points in the year, when we wanted them to bring their records in.

As a result of changing how we billed we got much closer to our clients. Pretty much becoming, as I had always wanted to, a true trusted advisor to them.

What services will you include as part of your monthly fixed fee to clients?

Once you have clarity on your reasons for introducing fixed fee billing, then it is time to decide which services will be part of the fixed monthly fees for clients. In Chapter 4 you were taken through a process to decide what services to offer your clients and how you were going to bundle your services into packages. It makes sense to include the services you have put in your packages as part of your monthly fixed-fee to the client. Anything extra to this, such as help to access finance, should be charged separately and at an appropriate time to when the work was carried out.

Health warning!

When you move to charging your clients a monthly fee, and give them visibility of their numbers via a cloud accounting system such as Xero/ Quickbooks/Freeagent, this will naturally set up an expectation that they will have more contact with your firm. If part of their fee includes their software subscriptions, whether you like it not, you will find that your firm will receive queries from your clients related to these software packages. If you decide, like many firms have, to offer 'unlimited telephone and email support' as part of their fixed fee to a client, be very careful how you price this in. If you don't make an allowance in a Client's fee for this service, then you are likely to be losing money with the increased amount of client queries your firm will be dealing with. You may find it to be financially healthier to qualify with both your clients and your staff exactly what 'unlimited telephone and email support' actually means. What is included and what isn't included.

When in the client's financial year do you start charging them a monthly fixed fee?

If your Client doesn't take bookkeeping from your firm, there is potentially a lag between when you start to do your first job for them and the start of their financial year. In an ideal world you will ask clients to pay their first monthly instalment in the first month of their financial year. Remember that as Guy found, moving to billing your clients via monthly instalments may fundamentally change your relationships with your clients. I.e. if your firm bills them monthly, they expect to hear from your firm monthly.

With new Clients you can set the expectation that their first monthly fee will be due in the first month of their new financial year. If your new Client is joining you part the way through their financial year, or has work left over from a previous financial year, then you have two options:

- Charge them for work in the current or past financial year after you have completed the work, then move to a monthly fixed fee on the 1st month of their new financial year.

- Add together the fee for work that needs to be done, plus the 1st year's fees. Then divide this by 12 to get their monthly fee for the next 12 months.

For example, Raj's new client had his quarter 4 VAT return, statutory year end accounts and corporation tax payment from the previous year left to do. So Raj charged his new client a one off fee to cover the work from the previous year, plus the monthly fee for the new financial year.

What technology will your firm use to automate invoicing and bookkeeping?

On the face of it moving to billing your clients a minimum of 12 times in the year, means potentially 12 times more invoicing and bookkeeping work. If your firm invests in some of the newer fintech and often cloud-based products, invoicing and bookkeeping work can be largely automated.

For example:

- Practice Ignition will automatically set up all your invoicing, reconciliation and billing via direct debit or credit card payments for a client in your preferred Cloud Accounting System (Xero/ Quickbooks/FreeAgent) at the point the client signs their proposal.

- GoCardless, a Direct Debit provider, will, once the Direct Debit mandate is signed, integrate directly with your chosen Cloud Accounting System. It then takes as little as one click of a button to reconcile all the Direct Debit payments which come into your account on a particular day.

How to persuade 'stuck' clients to move to monthly billing via Direct Debit

On the face of it, moving your firm's clients to billing monthly via Direct

Debit is a real win-win. You and your clients both preserve cash flow AND have transparency about what it is going to cost. But people being what they are, irrational creatures (See Chapter 1), some clients may not see the same benefits as your firm for making the switch. In fact, they may even refuse to make the change.

These are the choices available to you if someone refuses to make the move to monthly billing via Direct Debit:

- Exit them as a client. Your firm doesn't need to work with every client.

- Penalise them by giving them an eye-watering fee increase. Faced with a large increase, most clients will make the switch.

- Understand what their fears are, and demonstrate to them that these fears are unfounded or very unlikely to become reality.

- Explain to them how they will save time and money if they are billed monthly by Direct Debit.

In summary

The hardest part of moving from time-based billing to fixed fee billing which your client pays in equal monthly instalments, is making the mindset shift. It's not wrong to make higher profits if your clients are very happy with the value your firm's services provide.

The key to making a successful switch from time-based billing to fixed-fee billing in monthly instalments is to:

- Work out when in the client's financial year they will start paying the monthly fixed fee

- Pick software solutions which make the set up of the invoice and the bookkeeping of monthly payments automated as much as possible.

How to put up your fees for a large proportion of your firm's clients

Topics covered in this chapter:

- What stops us from implementing a fee increase for clients

- The step-by-step process to implement your fee increase

- How to implement the fee increase without losing a large proportion of your clients (unless you want to!)

- How to deal with clients whose fee is going to significantly increase

- How to deal with clients who push back on your proposed fee

Ask most small accountancy firm owners and they will tell you that their fees are too low, and they know they need to increase them. This chapter examines firstly, the reasons why there is this reticence to implement a fee increase. Then the chapter takes you through a step-by-step process in order to successfully implement a wide scale fee increase for your clients.

Can you relate to this scenario?

Simon looked at his accounts and his bank balance and felt sick to the core. His team were crying out for new resource, but there just wasn't the cash flow to merit a new member of the team. In fact, there wasn't the cash flow to merit Simon paying himself this month. He'd yet to break this news to his wife.

So where was it all going wrong? When he started the practice 3 years ago he had such high hopes for the future. He was going to be THE online cloud accounting firm. There was so much opportunity out there which he was going to grab. Having split from his previous firm he was now free to build a hyper-efficient cloud-based and client-centric practice. The type of practice his former stuck-in-their-ways partners just couldn't see the need to build.

In the early days of the practice, he'd gone out to market with bold claims and punchy pricing. With his name above the door and headline low pricing, he didn't find it hard to pick up clients. Two years ago he had seen the writing on the wall and moved away from his low-balled fees. Playing the low-fee game was a mug's game. But two years on, those first loyal clients; the ones who had backed him in his new venture, were crucifying his profits and cash flow. He would have been fine but for an expensive year. They'd needed new offices, had to pay off an expensive member of staff who hadn't worked out, a much higher than anticipated renewal cost for the firm's PI insurance... and so it went on.

He knew he needed to put up his fees for this core of legacy clients. But it didn't feel fair. After all, they had trusted him and backed him in the early days when all he had were good intentions and his previous good reputation.

Can you relate to Simon's story? Whilst it may not match exactly your journey, nearly every small accountancy firm has a problem with legacy clients paying too little. These clients may have come onboard before you read this book and realised your fees were too low. Or perhaps they were your very first few clients. The ones you brought in on a really low fee before you knew any better.

It's one thing to acknowledge you have a problem with some clients on too low a fee. It's another thing to actually raise their fee levels.

Conquer your fears

Our old friend the Amygdala starts to go into overdrive the moment you think about raising fees for your current clients. It's putting all sorts of fears, whether grounded or not, into your head. For example:

- What would happen if all your clients upped and left? Could you afford this to happen?

- Your clients will be angry with you, is this what you want?

- Have you really got the time to implement a fee increase, or would you be best used actually doing client work to bring in fees?

- You're not good with difficult conversations, you are going to make a hash of this...

- You're meant to be good with figures and running a business, wouldn't your client think less of you if you say you've mucked up their fees?

- Many of these clients are now your friends, is this how you treat a friend?

- Some of these clients will need their fees doubled or tripled, can I actually do this?

- You've tried to put up your fees before and it didn't work. Why do you think this time is going to be any different?

Before you can actually get started with putting up your fees you need to sort out the mind games in your head. (See Chapter 3) This means going beyond the irrational fears in your head and starting to think rationally. The first thing to do is write down a list of the fears that are in your head right now. How many of these are real fears?

☞ **Exercise:** Facing your fears

Remember, as in Chapter 3, these fears are just your Amygdala trying to keep you safe. However, some of your fears could be grounded in reality. It's these fears that you now need some careful thinking about.

Do the maths

The biggest fear you probably have is that too many of your clients will walk out the door when you propose their new fee level. Whilst in your head you know that many of these clients are either unprofitable or very low profitability, can you afford to lose the cash flow?

You may find the maths tell a different story.

The reality is that this core of legacy clients are likely to tick some or all of these:

- Take a disproportionate amount of time to service than your other clients;

- Be unprofitable or only just break even;

- Often be the last minute merchants when it comes to getting their records to you; and

- Be on the mental 'pain in the arse' list that your staff always have.

Case study: *Thomas*

When Thomas did the maths he found his core of 50 legacy clients (out of his 150 clients in total) contributed less than 15% of his turnover, and only 5% of his profit. As you can imagine, Thomas was shocked by the maths. When he took into account the extra software costs he was carrying to service these 50 legacy clients, the fees he was paying to an outsourcer, he could afford to almost ditch all of these clients overnight and not lose a penny in cash flow.

Despite the circulating fears in your head, the reality is that you are only going to lose a handful at most of your clients when you put your fees up. And these are the clients you probably want to lose!

Do a client portfolio analysis

When it comes to your clients there will be some clients who need an eye-watering increase, and yes, you will have these. But there will be some who only need a bit of a tweak to their pricing. Your strategy for handling these fee increases will be different.

If your fee increase is only going to be a nominal amount, i.e. £5-10 a month extra, or in line with inflation, you can probably get away with a letter to your client explaining the reasons for the fee increase and when it is going to take effect. For example:

" *Our costs, particularly wages and software costs, have increased, and so regrettably we need to put your fees up by a small amount...* **"**

Whereas if your fee increase is going to be material, e.g. over 50% increase, you will almost always need to treat the client as if they are a potential new client when you redo their fees for them.

But before you can work out who needs which strategy, you need to do a Client Portfolio Analysis for your firm. A Client Portfolio Analysis is where you look at exactly what each client has spent with you year by year for the last 5 years. The best way to do this is to produce a spreadsheet with this data on. (See Diagram 8.0)

	Sector	Structure of business	Lifecycle	Size	Services	Relationship Lead	Location	Potential to refer	Source
Client A	Creative	Partnership	Mature	Medium	"Done for you" + Bookkeeping	Simon	North London	High	Client G
Client B	Charity	Charity	Mature	Small	Value	Kiran	North London	Low	Bank A
Client C	Creative	Ltd	Mature	Medium	"Done for you" + Bookkeeping	Simon	North London	Medium	Client G
Client D	Contractor	Sole Trader	Mature	Small	Personal Tax Return	Simon	North London	Low	Friend
Client E	Creative	Ltd	Mature	Medium	"Done for you" + Bookkeeping	Simon	North London	High	Client G
Client F	IT	Ltd	Growth	Medium	"Done for you" + Bookkeeping + Management accounts	Kiran	West London	High	Bank A

Diagram 8.0: Example Client Portfolio Analysis

Step 1: Produce a spreadsheet of all your clients and what they have spent with you by year for the last 5 years.

Step 2: Identify the different types of clients, e.g. by sector, structure of business, stage of business lifecycle, source of business etc. See Table 8.1 for ideas of ways you can segment your data.

Segment	Examples
Sector	Food Retail (Baker, Grocer, Butcher), E-commerce only, Café/Restaurant, Service-based retail (hairdresser, dry cleaners, etc.), Product-based retail (book store, toy store, etc.)
Structure of business	Sole trader, Partnership, LLP, Ltd, Social Enterprise, Not for Profit, Charity
Business lifecycle stage	Not trading yet, start up, growth, mature, decline, dormant
Size	Big, medium, small
Services they take from us	Year End Accounts, Tax returns, VAT, Bookkeeping, Companies House Filing, Management Accounts, Virtual Finance Director, Business Planning, Tax Planning
Relationship Lead	Simon, Heather, Kiran, Joy
Location	Flitwick, Ampthill, Maulden, Bedford, Luton, Milton Keynes, Northampton, Silsoe, Barton-le-Clay
Potential to refer us	High, medium, low
Source	Existing client referral, bank manager referral, referral, website, word-of-mouth

Table 8.1: Ways in which an accountancy firm who specialises in retail businesses could segment their data in a Client Portfolio Analysis

Step 3: Identify which Client takes which service from the firm and record this on your spreadsheet.

Step 4: If not done already, identify on the spreadsheet who is the nominated contact or Relationship Lead for that client.

Step 5: Add to your spreadsheet, if you have the figures, the profitability for each Client per year.

Step 6: Identify a way of grading each Client which has meaning for you and your firm. Your grading will be closely aligned to your firm's plans and objectives.

Grade each Client A to D where:

A Important Client either because they are strategically important, pay a high fee or regularly give us client referrals, or something else which is relevant to your firm strategy

B Potential to become an important Client

C A small, but profitable Client who is unlikely to grow

D Unprofitable, tough to work with or poor at paying fees

Step 7: Interrogate your data. In particular, ask these questions of the data:

- Which Clients are unprofitable or barely profitable?

- Which Clients could probably take on more services from us?

- Which Clients are paying less than our current or planned future fee rates?

- Are there any trends for the most profitable Clients, biggest Clients or least profitable Clients?

Step 8: Produce a spreadsheet of all your clients impacted by the fee increase. On the spreadsheet detail:

- What they are paying now

- Minimum amount their fee needs to increase by

- Actual new fee agreed

👉 **Exercise:** Client Portfolio Analysis

Having clarity about the number of clients who need a fee increase will help you reduce the voices in your head predicting impending doom if you put in place a fee increase.

Identify the 'what's in it for clients?'

Just suppose for a moment that one of your biggest suppliers, be it your landlord or a software supplier or an outsourcer turned around to you and told you your fees were going up by 50%. You'd first of all be shocked, secondly want to know why, and thirdly start considering whether you would still be getting value from this supplier at this new cost level.

When you tell your clients about the fee increase, they are going to have exactly the same questions in their heads as you did. This means that you need to get your story together of why fees need to go up. But not just 'why', if possible, what extra value will you be able to give to your clients as a result of this fee increase? Or why you can't carry on giving this level of service at the fee they are paying?

Anticipate objections

Not everyone is going to be reasonable about their fees going up. There is no easy way to sugar-coat this, you ARE going to have some difficult conversations with some of your clients about their fee increase. The best way to deal with these is brainstorm all the objections you think you will receive with your team or coach. Then literally script up answers to these objections.

Make a plan to re-quote for all the affected clients

It's now time to decide when you are going to contact each of your affected clients. If you have to re-quote for a large proportion of your clients it is best to phase these conversations across 3, 6 or 12 months. By phasing your fee increase conversations it reduces the probability that you could lose too many of your clients in one go. The best time to re-quote for clients is 1-3 months before their financial year end. The reasons for this are multiple, for example:

- You have the opportunity to completely review their business and financial needs for their new financial year;

- This is the best time to pick up some ad hoc tax planning or advisory work for their new financial year; and

- Your current contract is probably due for renewal around about this time.

What about clients where you need to double or triple their current fee level?

There will be some clients whose fees will probably double or maybe even triple. Considering that these clients are probably the ones you are losing the most amount of money on, you would expect that you would start with these first. However, often the opposite is true. After all, this level of increase is always going to be a difficult conversation. Knowing what you know now about anchoring and mental accounting (See Chapter 1), these are the clients who are most likely to baulk at the fee increase you are proposing. Plus, it is probably highly embarrassing to tell your client that you've got their fee levels so wrong for so long. As a result you may never quite get around to having fee increase conversations with these clients.

The best way to treat these clients is to treat them as a new Lead. After all, considering the amount of profit you are making on these clients, how much is it really going to affect your bottom line if they take their business elsewhere?

For example, booking time in with each of these clients to do, wherever possible, a face-to-face meeting to do a complimentary review of their business affairs.

Make yourself accountable to the fee increase conversations you need to have

It's fairly easy to procrastinate on doing your fee increase conversations with clients. After all, no-one likes the thought of a difficult conversation. (Your friend the Amygdala again!) Or a client deciding to leave and not accept the new fee. Without someone, either within your firm or an external coach, keeping you accountable to your fee increase conversations, it becomes very easy to just never quite get around to doing them.

Case study: *Stuart*

Stuart knew he was undercharging his clients. As a result he was struggling to make any kind of living with his practice. Any income he did receive always seemed to be swallowed up by the monthly wages bill.

It had got to the point of no return. So, when a friend suggested buying his practice it was an offer he couldn't refuse. The offer to buy his practice spurred Stuart to finally getting around to having those fee increases he had never quite got around to in the last 2 years.

To help Stuart make the calls to clients he engaged the services of a coach to politely, but persistently, nag him to get these calls done. Within 2 months he had not only had all the fee increase conversations he needed to, but had added nearly £50k extra to the selling practice of his practice.

Being held accountable to what you need to do is a very personal thing. Not everything works for everyone. Here are some ideas which may work for you:

- Get someone in your team to book in meetings with all the clients whose fees you need to raise

- Add into your year-end accounts process a meeting with clients in month 9 or 10 of their financial year to talk about the year ahead, but also what their fee for the new financial year will be.

- Engage an external coach to hold you accountable to your fee increase plan

Summary

The biggest battle with fee increases for existing clients will NOT be your clients refusing to accept them, but conquering the fears in your head. Once your fears are conquered, it is time to do a client portfolio analysis and identify which clients need their fees increased. Then put together a plan to re-quote and speak, or write, to all the affected clients.

What now?

It's now time for you to get on with your intention to charge what your firm is really worth. Reading this book on its own without doing something won't help you get there. If you haven't already, go to The Accountants Millionaires' Club – http://www.accountantsmillionaire.club to download your Workbook.

If you know you need some extra help and accountability to implement the ideas in this book and sort out your pricing and charge what your firm is worth, come and join The Accountants Millionaires' Club.

We'd love to know how you are getting on in your journey to charge what your firm is really worth. Find us both on LinkedIn, Twitter or send us an email. (Our contact details are below).

Heather Townsend

heather@heathertownsend.co.uk

http://www.LinkedIn.com/in/heathertownsend

Twitter: @heathertowns

Ashley Leeds

ashley@excedia.co.uk

http://www.LinkedIn.com/in/ashleyleeds

Twitter: @ashleyleeds2

About The Accountants Millionaires' Club

The Accountants Millionaires' Club is a community, set of tools, regular events and resources for accountancy firm owners. (see http://www. accountantsmillionaire.club)

If you're breaking 6 figures and looking to profitably scale to the magic million pound mark, then The Accountants Millionaires' Club is designed specifically for you.

If you want to know whether the club can help your accountancy firm, then read what Graeme Trennick, Partner at Graeme Trennick and Co, had to say about his first month in the club.

" I first met Heather and Ashley at an event ran by Practice Ignition and I'll be honest I had reservations before attending as with the investment needed financially together with the plans that we already had in place; was the Accountant Millionaire's Club (AMC) right for me?

Well it didn't take me long to realise how much I needed this and I verbally committed on the day. I had once been on a coaching programme with phenomenal results but never one so specifically aimed at accountants and having listened to what was being said; challenged where I thought challenge was justified, I just felt they understood where I was at and where I wanted to be. I also acknowledged that yes I might; and I stress the word 'might' have made similar progress on my own, but it would have taken significantly longer.

Having now been in the programme for just over a month; it feels like longer, and having worked so closely alongside Ashley, I strongly doubt that I would have made this amount of progress. The amount of resources, assistance and advice has been nothing short of mind-blowing and even after this short space of time we have; in the last seven days alone:

1. *Attracted a client who have committed to fee just shy of £500 per month that we would have historically charged £200 per month*

2. *Have refined our internal processes; this has been happening since the start of the programme, to deliver a much better value added proposition for this same client in less time than it previously took us to look after similar clients at £200 per month*

3. *Have proposals out there that would more than double our clients paying*

over £300 per month including one where; subject to acceptance, would be in excess of £1,000 per month

These words don't go far enough to demonstrate the value the programme has added to our business and if I was you I wouldn't dare not join as other accountants have the same resources as me who have joined and together we are all growing stronger, quicker and you cannot afford to be left behind.

It's your choice, I made mine. **"**

Or hear what Naveed Mughal of Accurox said after being in the club for a year:

" Membership of the Accountants Millionaires' Club has truly transformed my practice. In fact in the last 6 months my turnover has grown by 184% with a net profit margin of 43%. I've calculated the ROI for my first year as a member is well in excess of 15 times.

When I first joined the club I was living hand to mouth with my cash flow, often having to dip in the money I had put aside to pay my VAT and corporation tax bill. After 6 months in the club I was able to stop worrying about cashflow as I now normally have 30-90 days of cash in the bank on top of the money I need to pay my VAT and corporation tax squirrelled away safely.

But probably the biggest difference has been to my confidence levels. Before I joined the club I knew I wanted to grow fast. I'm the sort of person where I will never be satisfied, and always will be wanting to grow faster or better. I'm now (mostly) much happier and have the confidence to take the right decisions when needed, instead of beating myself up and getting paralysed by indecision.

Working alongside Heather and learning from my other club members has helped me to minimise my confidence dips when I have faced setbacks, such as a team member leaving. But I've learnt to ask for a price which is in line with the value our firm brings to our clients. In fact, my time in the 'member spotlight', was probably worth £50-100k of extra turnover within 12 months of the conversation. You could say, it was the most profitable hour I'd ever spent.

Membership of the club has allowed me to build a community of experts around me who keep me grounded, focused and positive. Something I did not think was possible a year ago **"**

Why do Members join and stay?

Our members join and stay for many reasons, but these are the main reasons:

1. **We shortcut your journey to grow your firm**

" I have received so far so much support and training, it has literally cut my roll out time in half. I have been introduced to a wide array of potential partners, software solutions and general support that I have been able to make time to work on my business, take on new clients and support the embedded ones. I would absolutely recommend joining if you have any aspirations of growing your accountancy business as you will in the long term save yourself time and money. "

Lorna Leonard, Leonard Business Services

2. **We increase your firm's profit margin and capital value**

" My bank balance and happiness with my practice would now be SO much happier if I had taken action 12 months ago and joined the club then. "

Bob Evans, React Accountancy

" A very unexpected benefit was that within a month of being in the club I had saved over £10,500 by changing software suppliers and the impact of quoting and billing new clients at the right level. "

Paul Donno, 1Accounts

3. **We give you the clarity and confidence to make stuff happen and turn your aspirations into reality**

" The biggest difference has been to my confidence levels. Before I joined the club I knew I wanted to grow fast. I'm the sort of person where I will never be satisfied, and always will be wanting to grow faster or better. I'm now (mostly) much happier and have the confidence to take the right decisions when needed, instead of beating myself up and getting paralysed by indecision. "

Naveed Mughal, Accurox

4. **We keep you focused on the important stuff and give you the accountability to get things done.**

" Rather than thinking we needed to do everything at once, Heather got us to take ownership for the right actions to prioritise. She help us to account to implement. "

Adam Brodie, Ignition Financial

5. **We reduce your stress levels and working hours so you can do more of what you love**

" *With the accountability from the group accountability calls I am held to task and can really see me doing what is necessary to grow my practice.* **"**

Paul Donno, 1Accounts

What's included in your club membership

1:2:1 coaching every 3-6 months to help you focus on your growth plans: *Worth £600-3600 per year*

Having time to review and reflect to clarify your growth plans is essential if you are going to grow your firm. Every member of the club gets a minimum of 60 mins of 1:2:1 coaching every six months. GROW members get 60-90 mins every three months to help them review and revise their growth plans. Whereas, BOOST members get 3 hours every three months, as well as their normal 1:2:1 coaching session each month.

Fortnightly group coaching and accountability calls: *Worth £2,400+ per year*

Every fortnight GROW AND BOOST members are invited to a virtual group coaching and accountability call. In this 45-minute call you will have a chance to get help on your issues from other club members, as well as get accountability for your planned actions for the next two weeks.

3 members days a year (starting in 2020): *Worth £3,000 per year*

Our members days are where GROW and BOOST members can get together in person and network and mastermind with each other. (There is a small charge for SEED members) Members who have been in the club for over a year can bring a guest or staff member along for free.

6+ workshops a year: *Worth £900 per year*

All members are given complimentary tickets to our programme of workshops across the year.

Access to the club's Facebook Group: *Worth £475 per year*

The Club's private Facebook Group for members is a thriving group where members help each other, plus share resources and ideas.

On-going support from the Club's account managers: *Worth £2,400+ per year*

GROW and BOOST members have a telephone hot line to the club's account managers, whenever you just need a quick bit of help. (SEED members get email support rather than telephone support.) You are not alone when you are a member of the club.

Monthly 1:2:1 coaching for BOOST members: *Worth £3,600 per year*

Boost members get an hour of focused coaching each month, plus weekly check-ins and monitoring of their key KPIs each week.

Access to over 200+ resources in the club membership library: *Worth £3,000 per year*

Members get access to all the resources in the club membership site. The membership site grows by at least 3+ resources each month. In fact, new resources are normally built in response to member requests. Included within the membership library are new business scripts, process maps, marketing plans, recordings, role descriptions, tip sheets... and much, much more.

Access to 3-month CPD accredited mini training programmes: *Worth £2,500+ per year*

Every 3-4 months the club puts on a mini-training programme for members and/or their staff. Typically, the training programmes are 3-4 months in length and involve virtual masterclasses, group coaching calls and self-study. The training programmes have been designed so you can put them towards your CPD requirements, including verified CPD for the ACCA, for your institute.

Monthly live surgery sessions: *Worth £1,500 per year*

In the monthly live surgery sessions (which can be used for accredited CPD) you have the opportunity to quiz an advisory board member (or ordinary member who has done something well!) on some aspect of growing an accountancy practice which they have done well. Surgery sessions have included the following so far:

- How to do a fee increase
- How to grow a high performing team from scratch
- How to generate more referrals
- How to automate and systemise your practice
- How to win £3k+ clients every time

Monthly live member spotlights: *Worth £1,500 per year*

In the monthly member spotlight session you will be able to listen in (and ask questions) whilst a club member works on a specific issue they have. For example this could be:

- How to build a recruitment strategy for your firm
- How to automate your practice
- Pricing and pricing strategies
- How to reduce the time for Prospects to convert

Exclusive offers and discounts on software and other suppliers to the accountancy industry: *Worth £3000+*

Members get access to a range of discounts with 3rd party suppliers. We are adding more and more discounts over time. At the moment, members get the following discounts:

- 15% off a website build from PracticeWeb
- £400 credit with Global Infosys to help you get started with outsourcing year end accounts

- 10% off the first 12 months for new Practice Ignition users

- 50% off the first 4 months as a new Chaser partner

- New partners to Futrli get 25% off for 6 months (£300 discount)

- New and current partners to Futrli get 2 x Free Certifications

Total value: £22,000+ per year of membership

If you are ready to make your dream of growing a one million pound practice a reality, get in touch today.

The sooner you get started, the sooner you will get there.

Call Ashley on +44 (0) 1234 48 0123 or email ashley@excedia.co.uk

Printed in Great Britain
by Amazon